Creating AMERICAN JEWS

Historical Conversations About Identity

Edited by Karen S. Mittelman

D1716115

Published by the National Museum of American Jewish History, Philadelphia

In association with Brandeis University Press

Distributed by University Press of New England, Hanover and London

This catalogue has been published in conjunction with the exhibition,
CREATING AMERICAN JEWS.
Published by the National Museum of American Jewish History.
Distributed by the University Press of New England, Hanover, NH 03755

Library of Congress Catalog Card Number 98- 067380
ISBN 1-891507-01-X

Catalogue Design: Krohn Design
Photography: Will Brown
Printing: Hagerstown Bookbinding & Printing

*Brandeis Series in American Jewish
History, Culture, and Life*

Jonathan D. Sarna, Editor
Sylvia Barack Fishman, Associate Editor

*The Brandeis Series in American Jewish
History, Culture, and Life publishes
works that encompass all areas of
American Jewish civilization, including
history, religion, thought, politics,
economics, sociology, anthropology,
literature and the arts. Of particular
interest are interdisciplinary studies
that tie together divergent aspects
of the American Jewish experience.*

Contents

Foreword

The American Jewish experience is a big story. For the National Museum of American Jewish History, planning a core, permanent exhibition exploring this story has indeed been an exercise in deciding what kind of past we want our visitors to have, as well as the best ways to evoke that past for a broad audience. All history exhibitions, or history told in any medium, face a similar challenge of selection. We faced the additional challenge of making appealing and engaging a story that until recently has met with relatively limited attention and interest.

Why has American Jewish history fared so poorly in Hebrew schools, public schools, and even in Jewish studies departments, and with publishers? After all, it is an American story, and Americans are usually very proud of their past. But American Jewish history vies for limited space in a crowded curriculum. For Jews, Eastern Europe, Biblical times, and the Holocaust and Israel have drawn attention. For non-Jews, Jews in America are viewed as but one of many ethnic and religious groups that have peopled our nation.

The American Jewish experience, in comparison with the modern touchstones of Israel and the Holocaust, is perceived as lacking in drama and pathos, as historian Deborah Dash Moore has pointed out. But as visitors to CREATING AMERICAN JEWS will learn, stories of American Jewish life are evocative, moving, involving – and our own.

What is the best way to provide a sense of connection to the American Jewish experience for our visitors? Many museums, in presenting core exhibitions, have chosen to present a sweeping chronological narrative overview of their subjects. The staff and Board of the NMAJH decided on a very different approach. We chose to tell the stories of many individuals, most of them ordinary and unknown, and the choices that they made, as they created their identities as Americans and as Jews.

Our visitors will discover that the American Jewish experience has been, and continues to be, a rich and diverse tapestry. The identity of American Jews has been based on when they lived, the region and neighborhood they settled, where their grandparents and parents came from, whether they were Sephardic or Ashkenazic, observant or secular, male or female, young or old. But most of all, Jewish identity in America, has, for the first time in Jewish history, been based on choice. Jews in America have chosen whether to speak Yiddish or Ladino or English at home; to formally affiliate with a community; to attend a synagogue; to educate their children Jewishly; to support Israel. All of these choices have shaped their own personal and peculiar synthesis of what it has meant – and means today – to be at once Jewish and American.

The development of CREATING AMERICAN JEWS took place over many years, and depended on the expertise, creativity and commitment of many people, both inside and outside the National Museum of American Jewish History. First and foremost, thanks are due to Karen Mittelman, project director and the Museum's former exhibitions curator. Dr. Mittelman provided intellectual direction and rigor for a major, ambitious endeavor. She effectively led and inspired a team of staff and consultants, and also inspired trustees and funders. She produced an innovative and groundbreaking approach not only to the subject, but to history exhibitions generally. We are grateful, and wish her the best of luck in her new position at the National Endowment for the Humanities.

The initial planning team that Dr. Mittelman consulted included Lonnie Bunch, Barbara Kirshenblatt Gimblett, Jonathan Sarna, Jack Tchen, Morris Vogel and Jenna Weissman Joselit. We would like to thank each of them for engaging with us in the process of planning this exhibition. In 1993, Dr. Weissman Joselit exhorted us, "Complexity, divergence, dissension, passion…need be made an integral dimension." We hope that we have met her challenge.

Stephen Frank, who joined the Museum staff as Collections Curator in 1995, made arrangements for artifact conservation, and played a key role in the installation of the exhibition. Of even greater significance, his ideas and insights helped shape many aspects of the exhibition and the accompanying film. Kathleen Abplanalp, Curatorial Assistant, not only served as researcher par excellence, she stepped in to oversee installation of the exhibition upon Dr. Mittelman's departure. Charlotte Paul, Museum Educator, worked closely with Dr. Mittelman and the planning team to develop educational materials to accompany CREATING AMERICAN JEWS.

Thanks are also due to Development Director Sheila Raman, who wrote and produced the grant proposals that enabled us to achieve our ambitious fundraising goals. Public Relations Manager Jay Nachman developed the promotional materials that publicize the exhibition, as well as the accompanying public programs, and copy edited exhibition text and labels.

One of the great privileges that this project afforded the Museum was the opportunity to work with exhibition designer Jim Sims of Threshold Studio. Not only did Jim develop an extraordinarily creative design for CREATING AMERICAN JEWS, he made enormous contributions to the evolution of the exhibition concept. An equal privilege was working with filmmaker Andrea Simon, producer and director of "Promised Land: Jewish American Journeys." We are sure that her film will make the questions that the exhibition raises even more intriguing and inspiring.

Special thanks to the University Press of New England for the distribution of this catalogue, and to Jonathan Sarna, whose relationship with both the Press and the Museum made him an effective matchmaker.

The Museum's Board of Trustees, currently chaired by Dr. D. Walter Cohen, aided in the development of the project's content and the achievement of its financial goals. Edward H. Rosen, Matthew H. Kamens, Bubbles Seidenberg and Lyn M. Ross, who served as co-chairmen and past presidents of the Board were equally committed to CREATING AMERICAN JEWS. The Museum's Exhibitions Committee, ably chaired by Rhea Mandell, grappled with concept, design and text for several years. Our thanks to the entire committee, and especially to Mrs. Mandell, for their dedication and hard work.

An exhibition as major as this one clearly could not happen without significant financial support from generous donors. We would like to thank the William Penn Foundation, whose major support of the planning phases of this project enabled it to "get off the ground." The Lucius N. Littauer Foundation also supported planning and implementation costs of both the exhibition and the catalogue. Gifts in memory of Stephen A. Ritt, Jr. made it possible to conserve many artifacts in the exhibit. Kenneth J. Adelberg and the HiFi House Group of Companies provided invaluable assistance with audio-visual installations. The National Endowment for the Humanities funded an institutional self study in 1992, which enabled the staff to take the first steps in shaping the exhibit's interpretive direction.

We are grateful for major grants from the Maurice Amado Foundation and the Myer and Rosaline Feinstein Foundation. Additional support was received from the Pennsylvania Historial and Museum Commission; the Dolfinger-McMahon Foundation and the Pennsylvania Council on the Arts. The Pew Charitable Trusts have been significant supporters of the Museum's exhibitions and programs throughout the planning and implementation phases of this project. We would like to take this opportunity as well to acknowledge the late Etta Weinberg, whose gift in memory of her husband Bernard enabled the Museum to begin on the path to core exhibitions in 1977.

But most of all, we would like to thank the extraordinary leadership support of the trustees of the Samuel P. Mandell Foundation. Without their vision, commitment to Jewish education, and belief in CREATING AMERICAN JEWS, this project would not have come to fruition.

Margo Bloom
Director
National Museum of American Jewish History

What is the best way to provide a sense of connection to the American Jewish experience for our visitors? Many museums, in presenting core exhibitions, have chosen to present a sweeping chronological narrative overview of their subjects.

We chose to tell the stories of many individuals, most of them ordinary and unknown, and the choices that they made, as they created their identities as Americans and as Jews.

Acknowledgments

The making of this exhibition has been a journey in the truest sense. From the project team's free-wheeling discussions about the meanings of ethnic identity five years ago, to stimulating questions of design and interpretation, many people have helped to shape the journey, or to clear roadblocks.

My deepest thanks go to exhibition designer Jim Sims, whose exceptional creative spirit and sensitivity to interpretive issues have been an inspiration. His deep excitement about the project kept me going at times when I was frustrated, behind schedule or off track.

Andrea Simon asked questions that inspired us both, and created a film that beautifully captures the sense of exploration and passage at the heart of the exhibition.

Margo Bloom and Stephen Frank offered vital insights and advice throughout.

Associate curator Kathleen Abplanalp has helped to guide this project for three years. She made a significant intellectual contribution to the exhibition, as well as being a delight to work with.

Curatorial interns Rebekah Sobel, Rena Selya, Jared Fishman, Jordan Greenbaum and Laurie Siegel provided invaluable research into specific aspects of 20th century American Jewish identity. The artifact documentation of Ann Bonn, Claire Pingel and Judith Robins was also very helpful.

Kathleen and I relied on the generosity of numerous curators, archivists and librarians who were willing to search through their collections, measure artifacts, and fax us photographs, often on short notice. Special thanks to Kevin Profitt, American Jewish Archives; Nancy Hughes, Ellen Smith and Joellyn Wallen Zollman, American Jewish Historical Society; Jeanne Abrams, Beck Archives of Rocky Mountain Jewish History; Herman Hershman, Congregation Beth Sholom, Philadelphia; Anne Bond, Yanmin Huang, and Eric Paddock, Colorado Historical Society; Michael Stier, Corbis-Bettman Archives; Allen Reuben, Culver Pictures; Eleanor Gehres, Denver Public Library; Kim Ball, Georgia Historical Society; Richard Letterman and Gerald Spector, Har Zion Temple; Grace Grossman and Suzanne Kestner, Hebrew Union College Skirball Cultural Center and Museum; Phyllis Sichel, Dorothy Freedman and Claire Schweriner, Congregation Keneseth Israel; Anne Easterling, Museum of the City of New York; Diana De Santis, James Romero and Orlando Romero, Museum of New Mexico; Lee Arnold, Historical Society of Pennsylvania; Louise Cohen and Ruth Hoffman, Congregation Mikveh Israel, Philadelphia; Rabbi Arnold Belzer, Congregation Mickve Israel, Savannah and Nancy Birkheimer, Savannah Jewish Archives; Ron Potvin, Newport Historical Society; Harry Burton, New Market Press; John Kuss, New York Historical Society; Jesse Lankford, Jr.,North Carolina State Archives; Lily Schwartz, Philadelphia Jewish Archives Center; Elizabeth Bouvier, Supreme Judicial Court of Boston; Margaret Jerrido, Temple University Urban Archives; Susan Snyder, United States Holocaust Memorial Museum; and Charles Maynard and Stella De Sa Rego, University of New Mexico.

Rabbi Marcia Prager, Richard Siegel, Mike Tabor and Rabbi Arthur Waskow were generous with their time and their insights about the Jewish renewal movement. Eli Faber and Rabbi Albert Gabbai answered difficult research questions.

Bill Bound steered the project to completion, skillfully overseeing onsite fabrication and installation. I'm also deeply grateful to him, and to my son Jake, for enduring my long absences from home while I labored over the exhibition script.

Finally, I would like to thank several people who helped to make this catalog a reality. Jeanne Krohn created a richly-textured and elegant design for both the exhibition text and the book, and I'm happy to have had the opportunity to work with her. Amy Whitaker edited the manuscript with skill and sensitivity.

And it was a pleasure to work with Phyllis Deutsch and Nanine Hutchinson of the University Press of New England, who have made it possible for this catalog to reach a wider audience.

Introduction

> "Dear parents, I know quite well you will not like my bringing up my children as Gentiles. Here they cannot be brought up otherwise. Jewishness is pushed aside here . . . . You can believe me that I crave to see a synagogue to which I can go. The way we live now is no life at all."
>
> -Rebecca Samuel,
> Petersburg, Virginia, 1791

Karen S. Mittelman

For Rebecca Samuel, America was no Promised Land. Newcomers to the tiny town of Petersburg, she and her husband Hyman – also an observant Jew – despaired of being able to create a Jewish life on these shores. Many Jews, in fact, found themselves adrift in the New World, cut loose from the familiar anchors of communal identity. Their struggles and their dreams are recorded in eloquent letters sent across the Atlantic, wondering how Jewish life could survive in such a vast and alien place.

The crisis Rebecca Samuel faced in 1791 was met again and again by later generations of American Jews. In every century since the first Jews settled in New Amsterdam in 1654, American Jewish life has reached what appeared to be a critical juncture. The enticements of American culture, the force of the mainstream, and the tangible rewards of prosperity have repeatedly threatened to absorb everything distinctive about Jewish identity.

Usually, communal leaders have responded to such moments with extreme alarm, predicting the end of American Jewish life as they knew it. In every century including our own, there have been dire warnings about the waning of Jewish identity, symbolized by declines in synagogue attendance, relatively low Jewish birthrates and soaring rates of intermarriage.

As historians, we can see these moments instead as the creative sparks that have kept the community alive, moments when the variety and extravagant possibility inherent in American life (and Judaism) are laid bare. We can place such moments as part of a larger journey – the journey of American Jews to create themselves.

CREATING AMERICAN JEWS explores that journey. It is an exhibition that considers how Jews have adapted to America, inscribing their dreams and disappointments on the American landscape, from colonial times to the present. At its heart, it is about the impulse to reinvent ourselves that history has embedded in the Jewish soul.

The essays in this volume are reflections on the meanings of ethnic identity and community, themes that have undergone a thorough re-examination in the past decade in both popular and intellectual circles. The process of crafting an identity has become a subject of debate on prime time television as well as in scholarly journals, as Americans seek to understand what – at the deepest levels – connects us as a nation.

> The process of crafting an identity has become a subject of debate on prime time television as well as in scholarly journals, as Americans seek to understand what – at the deepest levels – connects us as a nation.

As "American" identity itself has come under scrutiny, ethnic historians are re-thinking the ways successive groups of immigrants defined themselves as Americans. Social historians have tended to neglect that process of Americanization, celebrating instead the strength of immigrant cultures and the tenacity of ethnic heritages. Recently, however, a new group of historians has begun to challenge this emphasis on ethnic persistence. Studies by David Gerber, Ewa Morawska and Kathleen Neils Conzen offer a fresh look at the interactions between immigrant cultures and changing "American" norms and values.[1]

Increasingly, scholars have come to see cultural identity as something that is worked out again and again – an ongoing creative struggle, reinvented by each generation. Cultural markers of identity that are rejected by one generation resurface with renewed power and a transformed meaning for a later generation confronting a different America. Not only time, but also factors such as gender, age, and geographic region profoundly complicate the meeting of American and ethnic ways of life. In short, ethnic affiliations have proven to be far more dynamic and malleable than we had imagined.

The essays in CREATING AMERICAN JEWS consider ethnic identity as an ongoing process of cultural invention. At the heart of our exploration of identity is the question of how individuals in the past have understood and articulated their own sense of "being Jewish in America," and how that sense has evolved over time.

Jonathan Sarna's examination of synagogue culture in the era of the American Revolution reveals that passionate conflicts about the nature of American Jewish identity are not new. As early as the 1790s, Jews chafed against the restraints of the traditional synagogue-community. New ideals of liberty and democracy embodied in the Revolution challenged Jews to reinvent community, to rewrite the laws governing their synagogues, and to build alternatives to the traditional communal structures that had defined them as a religious group. Incorporating the democratic vocabulary of the Bill of Rights, new synagogue constitutions affirmed the essential equality of all (male) Jews in the community and gave each an equal voice in governing the community.

Yet Sarna also tells us that the new democratic rhetoric of the Revolution was hard to live up to; too much freedom threatened to endanger the stability of the synagogue-based community. Jews had joined a struggle essential to the American spirit in the early 19th century – the struggle to balance community and spiritual individuality, authority and liberty, tradition and change.

William Toll's essay reminds us of the power of place in shaping Jewish identity in the mid-19th century. Lured by the promise of cheap land and social and economic opportunity, Jewish settlers in the West encountered a different America than those who made their living in the cities and towns of the Northeast or the South. Emigrating from Central Europe, these men and women carved out a prominent place for themselves as members of an elite merchant class with a solid sense of civic responsibility. In the relatively open social atmosphere of the Western territories, Jews were key to developing the political, moral and civic life of their hometowns – serving on school boards and militias and as mayor and chief of police – while at the same time founding B'nai B'rith lodges, Hebrew Benevolent associations and synagogues, which nurtured a distinctive Jewish identity on the frontier.

Perhaps more than any other generation, the Eastern European immigrants who arrived between 1881 and 1914 had to mold a new Jewish identity around – and in spite of – the allure and the energy of American culture. No central communal authority existed to define the contours of Jewish life, and the possibilities offered by America seemed limitless. For this generation and especially their children, Jewishness increasingly came to be defined as a matter of sentiment. As they shed their parents' Yiddish inflection, their Old World coats and shawls, all the accoutrements of otherness, second generation Jews were left with a Jewish identity that resided largely in their hearts and minds. As one emphatically modern New Yorker explained in 1941, "We have to see to it that our children grow up as Jews and this has nothing to do with religious ceremonies...One must be a Jew in his heart." [2]

Jenna Weissman Joselit's essay probes the new rhetoric of romance – an essentially American language – which the sons and daughters of immigrants adopted to express a new sense of belonging to America. Skillfully analyzing three cultural moments in the early to mid-20th century, Joselit argues that as Jews embraced the promise of the "melting pot" they were simultaneously articulating a new understanding of Jewish identity. Far from simply assimilating, second generation Jews fused American ideals of liberty and personal happiness with their own particular brands of Jewish culture and belief, creating an insistently modern and exuberantly American Jewish identity.

As the foregoing essays demonstrate, the survival of American Jewish identity has demanded constant negotiations between old and new, between changing traditions and the fluid promises of American culture. Jewishness in America has become something that Rebecca Samuel certainly would not recognize, and indeed, something that makes many Jews in the 1990s uneasy. The evolution of the idea that to be Jewish is a choice – an idea that is still hotly contested in Orthodox circles – is the subject of David Hollinger's essay.

Hollinger describes a wholesale redefinition of Jewish ethnicity in America in the decades following World War II. The unequalled social and economic openness of postwar America, which vaulted Jews into the American mainstream, also posed a threat to Jewish distinctiveness. At the same time, Jews became enmeshed in a new discourse about ethnic identity, beginning in the 1980s, which redefined their position ideologically and politically *vis a vis* other American ethnic groups. Jews were grouped together with "European-Americans," in an ethno-racial model that gave primacy to race over religion. Hollinger argues persuasively that in the midst of this new division of ethnic territory, Jews have lost claim to the defining feature that has historically been most central to our uniqueness as a people – religion.

The new model, furthermore, emphasizes aspects of identity that are not central to Jewishness – race and color – and de-emphasizes linguistic differences, which have often set Jews apart. The conspicuous absence of Jewish Americans from most contemporary discussions of multiculturalism and diversity has deprived Jews of a forum for affirming their identity as Jews and as Americans.

The effect of the situation that Hollinger describes is to throw the gates wide open to any kind of Jewish practice, any form of affiliation, any ritual or belief that someone defines as Jewish. Jewish identity in America today cannot be automatically assumed or ascribed – it begs to be invented, to be wrestled with and made new. What caused Rebecca Samuel to despair two centuries ago has become our adventure – the adventure of creating Jewish identity. Remaking ourselves into American Jews, we cannot help but remake America.

Jewish identity in America today cannot be automatically assumed or ascribed— it begs to be invented, to be wrestled with and made new.

1. Russell A. Kazal, "Revisiting Assimilation: The Rise, Fall, and Reappraisal of a Concept in American Ethnic History," *American Historical Review* (April 1995) 437-471.

2. I. Steinbaum, "A Study of the Jewishness of Twenty New York families," *YIVO Annual* vol. 5, 1950.

The Revolution in theAmerican Synagogue

Jonathan D. Sarna

I n 1654, twenty-three Jews – men, women and children, refugees from Recife, Brazil, which Portugal had just recaptured from Holland – sailed into the Dutch colony of New Amsterdam on a vessel named the Sainte Catherine. This marked the beginning of American Jewish history, as we know it.

What distinguished these bedraggled refugees was their desire to settle down permanently. Jews who had landed in North America earlier, one as early as 1585, had no intention of forming a community; all had quickly departed. Now, for the first time, families of Jews had arrived. Their hope was "to navigate and trade near and in New Netherland, and to live and reside there." [1]

Peter Stuyvesant, the dictatorial Director-General of New Netherland, sought permission to keep the Jews out. The Jews, he explained in a letter to his superiors, were "deceitful," "very repugnant," and "hateful enemies and blasphemers of the name of Christ." He asked the Directors of the Dutch West India Company to "require them in a friendly way to depart" lest they "infect and trouble this new colony." He warned in a subsequent letter that, "giving them liberty we cannot refuse the Lutherans and Papists." Stuyvesant understood that the decisions made concerning the Jews would serve as precedent and determine the colony's religious character forever after. [2]

Back in Amsterdam, "the merchants of the Portuguese [Jewish] Nation" sent the directors of the Dutch West India Company a carefully worded petition that listed reasons why Jews in New Netherland should *not* be required to depart. One of these reasons doubtless stood out among the others: "many of the Jewish nation are principal shareholders" in the company. The directors pointed to this fact, as well as to the "considerable loss" that Jews had sustained in Brazil, and ordered Stuyvesant to permit Jews to "travel," "trade," "live," " and "remain" in New Netherland, "provided the poor among them shall not become a burden to the company or to the community, but be supported by their own nation." After several more petitions, Jews secured the right to trade throughout the colony, serve guard duty, own real estate, and worship in private. [3]

A decisive moment in the religious life of the nascent Jewish community of North America came in 1655 when a borrowed Torah scroll, garbed in a "green veil, and cloak and band of India damask of dark purple color," arrived from Amsterdam. The handwritten parchment text of the Pentateuch is Judaism's central and most sacred ritual object, and its reading forms a focal point of Jewish group worship. In

A decisive moment in the religious life of the nascent Jewish community of North America came in 1655 when a borrowed Torah scroll, garbed in a "green veil, and cloak and band of India damask of dark purple color," arrived from Amsterdam.

Colonial North America, as elsewhere, it was the presence of a Torah scroll that served as a defining symbol of Jewish communal life and culture, of Jewish law and lore. It created a sense of sacred space: elevating a temporary habitation into a cherished place of holiness, and the private home in which Jews worshipped into a hallowed house of prayer. As long as the Torah was in their midst, the Jews of New Amsterdam knew that they formed a Jewish religious community. The green veiled Torah was returned to Amsterdam about 1663, signifying that the community had now scattered. The *minyan*, the prayer quorum of ten males over the age of thirteen traditionally required for Jewish group worship, could no longer be maintained.[4]

The subsequent reappearance of Torah scrolls in the city, which was now under the British, signaled that the community had been reestablished; private group worship resumed. Wherever Jews later created communities in North America, in Savannah and Newport for example, they brought Torah scrolls with them. In smaller eighteenth-century colonial Jewish settlements, such as Lancaster and Reading, where Judaism was maintained for years by

Torah scroll sent to Savannah in 1737

Congregation Mickve Israel, Savannah

dedicated laymen without a salaried officiant or a formal synagogue, the Torah scroll functioned in a similar way. It embodied the holy presence around which Jewish religious life revolved.

Back in New Amsterdam, now renamed New York, the British, in an effort to promote tranquility and commerce, scrupulously maintained the religious status quo, according Jews the same rights (but no more) as they had enjoyed under the Dutch. The operative British principle, for Jews as for other social and religious deviants from the mainstream, was "quietness." As long as Jews practiced their religion "in all quietness" and "within their houses," the authorities generally left them in peace. When, in 1685, the approximately twenty Jewish families in town petitioned for the right to worship in public, they were summarily refused; "publique Worship," they were informed, "is Tolerated... but to those that professe faith in Christ." [5]

Around the turn of the eighteenth century, public worship became available to Jews without any fanfare or known change in the law. Kahal Kadosh Shearith Israel ("the Holy Congregation Remnant of Israel") became the official name of North America's first synagogue. That name, like the names of many other early synagogues in the New World, hinted at the promise of redemption (see Micah 2:12). It recalled the widespread belief that the dispersion of Israel's remnant to the four corners of the world heralded the ingathering. The synagogue also closely resembled its old world counterparts in that it functioned as both the traditional synagogue and the organized Jewish community, or *kehillah*. It assumed responsibility for all aspects of Jewish religious life: communal

Drawing of "Jew's Synagogue" by William Strickland, architect. Philadelphia, 1824

Congregation Mikveh Israel

worship, dietary laws, life-cycle events, education, philanthropy, ties to Jews around the world, oversight of the cemetery and the ritual bath, even the baking of matzah and the distribution of Passover *haroset*. Functionally speaking, it was equivalent to the established colonial church. It was monopolistic, it disciplined those who violated its rules (usually through fines, but sometimes with excommunication), and it levied assessments (essentially taxes) on all seatholders. Unlike established churches, however, the synagogue-community had no legal standing in the colonies. Jews were not required to join it nor did state funds support the congregation. Nevertheless, the synagogue-community saw itself, and was seen by others, as the Jews' representative body – it acted in their name – while the synagogue served as a central meeting and gathering place for local Jews.

The events in New York served as the model for other organized Jewish communities that took root in the American colonies – Savannah (1733), Newport (1750s), Charleston (1750s), and Philadelphia (1760s). These four communities developed in tidewater settlements, with mixed urban populations, where Jews found economic opportunity and a substantial measure of religious toleration. Savannah's Jewish colonial community was the earliest, the shortest-lived and the most distinctive. There, in a bid to become self-supporting, forty-two Jews arrived from England on July 11, 1733. They were sponsored by London's Sephardic community, as part of a colonization effort that was characterized by historian Jacob Rader Marcus as inspired by an "amalgam of patriotism, philanthropy, expediency, and concern for their fellow Jews." [6] The colonialists carried with them a Torah and other religious articles "for the use of the congregation that they intended to establish." They won the right to settle and trade (thanks, in part, to the Jewish

Freedom and democracy, as we understand them, were unknown in colonial synagogues. Jews of that time would have viewed such revolutionary ideas as dangerous to Judaism and to the welfare of the Jewish community as a whole.

physician Dr. Samuel Nuñez, who stopped the spread of a ravaging disease),
received generous land grants, and were soon joined by other Jews seeking
their fortune in the New World – Sephardim as well as Ashkenazim. Group
worship in a private house began at once, the Sephardim apparently
dominating, and two years later, according to a surviving diary, Jews met "and
agreed to open a Synagouge [sic]… named K.-K. Mikva Israel," which was
organized on the model of a synagogue-community.[7] In 1740, however, the
threat of a Spanish invasion frightened the Sephardic Jews away – they knew
what awaited them if Spain won – and a Torah that had been used in Savannah
was forwarded to New York. Three Jewish families remained in town
worshipping individually, but the congregation did not resume meeting – at a
private home – until 1774. Thereafter, while Sephardic tradition predominated,
the lay leaders of Savannah's Jewish community were Ashkenazim.[8]

*Interior of Touro
synagogue in
Newport, RI*

John Hopf Photography

Newport, Charleston and Philadelphia developed along different lines.
In all three cities there had been multiple attempts to organize and establish
regular synagogue worship, dating back, in Newport, to the seventeenth
century. Success came only in the second half of the eighteenth century,
however, as the number of Jews in the American colonies increased to nearly
one thousand, and colonial cities prospered. Shearith Israel extended help to
these fledgling congregations, and all three followed its lead in organizing as a
synagogue-community, embracing Sephardic traditions, and welcoming Jews of
diverse origin, including Ashkenazim, into their midst. Prior to the Revolution,
Jews in Charleston and Philadelphia lacked both the money and the confidence
to invest in a permanent house of worship, and so worshipped in private
homes and rented quarters. The wealthy Jews of Newport, by contrast,
exhibited great confidence in their surroundings. With financial assistance from
Jews in New York, London and the West Indies, they built a beautiful

synagogue, which they dedicated in 1763. Now known as the Touro Synagogue, it
is the oldest surviving synagogue structure in North America.

The synagogue-community, as it developed in the major cities where Jews
lived, proved to be an efficient means of meeting the needs of an outpost Jewish
community. It promoted group solidarity and discipline and it evoked a sense of
tradition as well as a feeling of kinship toward similarly organized synagogue-
communities throughout the Jewish world. It also enhanced the chances that even
small clusters of Jews, remote from the wellsprings of Jewish learning, could
survive from one generation to the next.

Freedom and democracy, however, did not loom large among the values
espoused by the synagogue community. It stressed instead the values of tradition
and deference as critical to the Jewish community's wellbeing. These values had
stood Sephardic Jews in good stead for generations, and even though Sephardic
Jews no longer commanded a majority among eighteenth-century colonial
American Jews, their values still ruled supreme. At Shearith Israel in New
York, for example, tradition loomed so large that various prayers were
recited in Portuguese and the congregation's original minutes were
written in Portuguese (with an English translation) – even
though only a minority of the members understood that
language and most spoke English on a regular basis. But
Portuguese represented tradition; it was the language of the
community's founders and of the Portuguese Jewish Nation
scattered around the world. Ladino, or Judeo-Spanish,
written in Hebrew letters, was only spoken by the
Sephardim of the Ottoman Empire. In matters of worship,
too, Shearith Israel closely conformed to the traditional
minhag (ritual) as practiced by Portuguese Jews in Europe
and the West Indies. Innovations were prohibited; "our
duty," Sephardic Jews in England (writing in Portuguese)
once explained, is "to imitate our forefathers." [9] On a deeper
level, Sephardic Jews believed, as did the Catholics they had
lived among for so long, that ritual could unite those whom life
had dispersed. They wanted members of their Nation to feel at home
in any Sephardic synagogue anywhere in the world: the same liturgy, the
same customs, even the same tunes.

Deference, too, formed part of Sephardic tradition. Members of the
community expected to submit to the officers and elders of the congregation. These
were generally men of wealth and substance who took on the burden of communal
leadership out of a sense of *noblesse oblige* and who perpetuated one another in
office. There were disagreements, but there was also a consensus that disobedience
to authority should be punished. In 1746, for example, members of Shearith Israel
decreed that obstreperous worshippers be asked to leave the synagogue and not
return until they paid a fine. They explicitly included themselves in the edict "if
wee do not behave well." [10] In 1760, they severely punished Judah Hays for
disobeying the congregation's *parnas* (president), even though Hays was a
significant member. As late as 1790, Savannah Jews wrote into their synagogue
constitution a requirement that "decent beheavour [sic] be observed by every
person during service," and warned that offenders, "on being called to order and
still persisting, shall, for every such offence, pay a fine not exceeding forty
shillings."[11] In enforcing discipline through such edicts, Jews were following both
the teachings of their ancestors and the practices of their non-Jewish neighbors.
Indeed, deference to those in authority and to those who held the largest 'stake in

society' was accepted by "the bulk of Americans" in the mid 18th century.[17] By contrast, freedom and democracy, as we understand them – the right to dissent, the right to challenge the leadership in a free election, the right to secede and establish a competing congregation, the right to practice Judaism independently – were unknown in colonial synagogues. Jews of that time would have viewed such revolutionary ideas as dangerous to Judaism and to the welfare of the Jewish community as a whole.

The American Revolution, however, legitimated precisely these revolutionary ideas. In rebelling against the British, the colonists explicitly rejected both tradition and deference, and they overthrew many of the established ideologies that had previously governed their existence under the British. These changes were by no means confined to politics; they also affected the realm of religion. Religious establishments throughout the former colonies were overthrown, religion and state were separated, and democracy became an important religious value. As a result hierarchic churches waned in popularity and democratic ones, like Methodism, became more popular.

Judaism too was transformed by the Revolution. A majority of Jews supported the Revolution, including the *chazan* (minister) of Shearith Israel, Gershom Seixas, who left the city with his followers in the face of the British occupation forces. After the Revolution, in all of the communities where Jews lived, patriotic Jews returned to their synagogues and very soon had to grapple with the new situation in which they found themselves. The challenge they faced was whether Judaism as they knew it could be reconciled with freedom and democracy. Could Jews maintain the structure of the traditional synagogue-community that bound them together and promoted group survival, and at the same time accommodate new political and cultural realities? In an initial effort to meet this challenge, every American synagogue rewrote its constitution. More precisely, they wrote *constitutions* for the first time; they had previously called their governing documents *askamot* or *haskamot*, meaning agreements or covenants. The new documents broke from the old Sephardic model, incorporated large dollops of republican rhetoric, and provided for a great deal more freedom and democracy – at least on paper. At New York's Congregation Shearith Israel, in 1790, a particularly interesting constitution was promulgated, the first that is known to have contained a formal "bill of rights." The new set of laws began with a ringing affirmation of popular sovereignty suggestive of the American Constitution: "We the members of the K.K. Shearith Israel." Another paragraph explicitly linked Shearith Israel with the "state happily constituted upon the principles of equal liberty, civil and religious." Still a third paragraph, the introduction to the new bill of rights (which may have been written at a different time) justified synagogue laws in terms that Americans would immediately have understood:

> Whereas in free states all power originates and is derived from the people, who always retain every right necessary for their well being individually, and, for the better ascertaining those rights with more precision and explicitly, frequently from [form?] a declaration or bill of those rights. In like manner the individuals of every society in such state are entitled to and retain their several rights, which ought to be preserved inviolate.
>
> Therefore we, the profession [professors] of the Divine Laws, members of this holy congregation of Shearith Israel, in the city of New York, conceive it our duty to make this declaration of our rights and privileges.[13]

Could Jews maintain the structure of the traditional synagogue-community that bound them together and promoted group survival, and at the same time accommodate new political and cultural realities?

In an initial effort to meet this challenge, every American synagogue rewrote its constitution.

The new bill of rights explicitly ended many of the colonial-era distinctions between members and non-members. It did so by declaring that "every free person professing the Jewish religion, and who lives according to its holy precepts, is entitled to... be treated in all respect as a brother, and as such a subject of every fraternal duty."[14] The new system also made it easier for members of the congregation to attain synagogue office. Leadership no longer rested, as it had for much of the colonial period, with a self-perpetuating elite.

An even more democratic constitution was produced in 1789 by the fledgling Jewish community of Richmond, Virginia. The document began with a democratic flourish: "We, the subscribers of the Israelite religion resident in this place, desirous of promoting the divine worship...." It then offered membership and voting privileges to "every free man residing in this city for the term of three months of the age of 21 years... who congregates with us." It tried to ensure "an equal and an independent representation" to everyone involved in synagogue government, and allowed even a single dissenting member to bring about a "meeting of all the members in toto" to pass on proposed rules and regulations. [15]

Most of these constitutions were subsequently modified, and some patterns from the past were reasserted, as the age-old values of the synagogue-community and the new values of the fledgling republic proved hard to reconcile. In Charleston, to take an extreme example, the revised synagogue constitution of 1820 returned "all the functions formerly exercised by the people at large" to a self-perpetuating "general adjunta." [16] In New York and Philadelphia too, the synagogue-community was losing its religious hold, and its confidence. The strategy of promoting Judaism through tradition and through a single overarching institution that would unify all Jews was crumbling under the weight of demands for more freedom and democracy. In his study of American Christianity during this period, the religious historian Nathan Hatch found that "The American Revolution and the beliefs flowing from it created a cultural ferment over the meaning of freedom. Turmoil swirled around the crucial issues of authority, organization, and leadership." For Jews and Christians alike in the United States, "the first third of the nineteenth century experienced a period of religious ferment, chaos and originality unmatched in American history." [17]

Young Jews moved to transform and revitalize their faith, somewhat in the spirit of the Second Great Awakening. In so doing they hoped to thwart Christian missionaries, who insisted that in order to be modern one had to be Protestant, and they sought most of all to bring Jews back to active observance of their religion.

The "Hebrew Congregations" wrote letters of congratulation to the President in 1790, expressing the confidence Jews felt in their new republic.

Letter of reply, George Washington to the Hebrew Congregations of Philadelphia, New York, Charleston and Richmond, 1790

Congregation Mikveh Israel, Philadelphia

Two telling examples illustrate the kinds of challenges that synagogue-communities now faced. In New York, in 1813, the *shohet* (ritual slaughterer) of Shearith Israel decided to reject the congregation's terms of employment and to sell kosher meat independently. This represented deliberate and unprecedented defiance of the congregation's authority in a matter of critical Jewish concern. The congregation, seeking to reassert its authority, promptly used its political connections with the New York Common Council to pass an ordinance that "no Butcher or other person shall hereafter expose for sale in the public Markets any Meat sealed as Jews Meat who shall not be engaged for that purpose by the Trustees of the congregation of Sheerith Israel." Once upon a time this would have meant the end to the story (except that perhaps the congregation might have disciplined the independent-minded *shohet* as well). Now, however something remarkable happened that had never happened before. Eight members of the congregation, supporters of the dissident *shohet*, protested to the New York Common Council that this Ordinance "impair[ed]" their "civil rights," was "an encroachment on our religious rites [sic] and a restriction of those general privileges to which we are entitled." They asked that the ordinance be "immediately abolished" and privately complained that it was "an infringement on the rights of the people."[18] The language itself was revealing, for it resonated with the rhetoric of liberty and freedom that pervaded American life at the time. The result, however, was even more revealing. The Common Council, unwilling to enter into what it now understood to be an internal Jewish dispute, expunged its original ordinance, and washed its hands of the whole matter. This response signaled a sharp diminution of the "established" synagogue's authority. Henceforward, in New York, the synagogue-community's authority over kosher meat was completely voluntary; local Jews had established their right to select a *shohet* of their own choosing. Though they did not immediately exercise that right, this episode was a harbinger of the greater challenges the synagogue-communities were to face.

This prayer of gratitude for the new nation was recited in Richmond's synagogue in 1789.

National Museum of American Jewish History, Gift of ARA Services, Inc., through the agency of William S. Fishman

Meanwhile, in Charleston, which in the immediate post-Revolutionary era was the largest Jewish community in the United States, the authority of the synagogue community was also being challenged – indeed, repeatedly. There were short-term schisms, a memorable brawl in 1811, and most revealingly, an unprecedented movement to establish private Jewish cemetery plots. The Tobias family established one, so did the da Costa family, and a larger private cemetery was established on Hanover Street in Hampstead by half a dozen Jewish dissidents, including Solomon Harby. Beth Elohim, Charleston's established synagogue, attempted to ban this practice, for it undermined a critical pillar of its authority, the threat of withholding Jewish burial from those who either defaulted on their obligations or were "rejected" by the congregation. "There shall be one Congregational Burial Ground only..." the congregation's 1820 constitution proclaimed, although in the interests of peace it provided "that this law shall not extend to any family place of interment already established."[19] But like so many other attempts to reassert congregational authority over independent-minded dissidents, this one too failed. In these post-Revolutionary decades, in both synagogues and churches, we see burgeoning religious ferment, challenges to established communal authority, and appeals to American values to legitimate expressions of religious dissent.

All of this set the stage for the religious revolution that transformed American Judaism in the 1820s, a remarkable era in American Jewish history that paralleled in American history the epochal period of the Second Great Awakening and the beginning of the Jacksonian age.[20] At this time, the Jewish community was still small – three to six thousand – but more Jews than ever before were native-born and the number of immigrants from Western and Central Europe was growing. This was a decade during which a significant number of Jews began moving to the West. It was also a decade that saw a few extraordinary Jews emerge in American cultural and political life, and a decade that witnessed the first serious writings by American Jews on Judaism – largely polemical and apologetic pieces designed to counter Christian missionaries. It was during this time that Jews became seriously alarmed about what we would call "Jewish continuity." In New York, Charleston and Philadelphia, Jews expressed concern about Jewish religious indifference – what those in Charleston called the "apathy and neglect" manifested toward Judaism by young and old alike. They worried about the future. "We are... fallen on evil times," Haym M. Salomon, son of the Revolutionary-era financier wrote to the *parnas* of Shearith Israel.[21] While many of his complaints focused on religious laxity, the real question, not quite articulated, was whether the colonial system of Judaism – one established traditional Sephardic synagogue per community – could adequately meet the needs of young Jews. These were people born after the Revolution, who were caught up in the heady, early nineteenth-century atmosphere of freedom, democracy, and religious ferment. Responding to this larger challenge, young Jews moved to transform and revitalize their faith, somewhat in the spirit of the Second Great Awakening. In so doing they hoped to thwart Christian missionaries, who insisted that in order to be modern one had to be Protestant, and they sought most of all to bring Jews back to active observance of their religion.

The immediate result of this revitalization effort was the final disestablishment of the synagogue-community in the two largest American Jewish communities of that time, New York and Charleston. In New York, a group of ambitious young Jews, mostly from non-Sephardic families, petitioned Shearith Israel's leaders for the seemingly innocuous right to establish their own early worship service "on the Sabbath mornings during the summer months."[22] The request brought into the open an assortment of communal tensions – young vs. old, Ashkenazim vs. Sephardim, newcomers vs. old-timers, innovators vs. traditionalists – that had been simmering within the congregation since the death of Gershom Seixas in 1816. First, there was an ugly dispute concerning the pension rights due the *chazan's* widow. Then the synagogue was unsettled by the arrival of new immigrants who sought to revitalize the congregation and in the process threatened to transform its very character. Meanwhile, shifting residential patterns drove many far from the synagogue; members wanted a congregation closer to

These were people born after the Revolution, who were caught up in the heady, early nineteenth-century atmosphere of freedom, democracy, and religious ferment.

where they lived. Sundry attempts to discipline those who violated congregational customs only added fuel to this volatile mix, and as passions rose synagogue attendance plummeted. With the proposed early morning service threatening to disrupt synagogue unity still further, the trustees "resolved unanimously... that this [petition] can not be granted." An accompanying "testimonial" warned that the proposed service would "destroy the well known and established rules and customs of our ancestors as have been practised... for upwards of one hundred years past."

Rather than abandoning their plan for a new worship service, the young people gathered "with renewed arduor [sic] to promote the more strict keeping of their faith," [24] and – urged on by Seixas' own son-in-law, Israel B. Kursheedt – formed an independent society entitled *Hebra Hinuch Nearim*, dedicated to the education of Jewish young people. The society's constitution and bylaws bespeak the spirit of revival, expressing "an ardent desire to promote the study of our Holy Law, and... to extend a knowledge of its divine precepts, ceremonies, and worship among our brethren generally, and the enquiring youth in particular." Worship, according to this document, was to be run much less formally than at Shearith Israel. There was to be time set aside for explanations and instruction, there was to be no permanent leader and, revealingly, there were to be no "distinctions" made among the members. The overall aim, leaders explained in an 1825 letter to Shearith Israel, was "to encrease [sic] the respect of the worship of our fathers." [25]

In these endeavors, we see familiar themes from the general history of American religion in this era: revivalism, challenge to authority, a new form of organization, anti-elitism, and radical democratization. Given the spirit of the age and the availability of funding, it is no surprise that the young people boldly announced "their intention to erect a new Synagogue in this city." It was to follow the "German and Polish minhag [rite]" and be located "in a more convenient situation for those residing uptown." [26] On November 15th, the new congregation applied for incorporation as B'nai Jeshurun, New York's first Ashkenazic congregation. [27]

As if conscious of the momentous step they were taking, the leaders of the congregation took pains to justify their actions on both American and Jewish grounds. First, they observed that "the wise and republican laws of this country are based upon universal toleration giving to every citizen and sojourner the right to worship according to the dictate of his conscience." Second, they recalled that "the mode of worship in the Established Synagogue [note the term!] is not in accordance with the rites and customs of the said German and Polish Jews." [28] Together, these two arguments undermined the basis for the synagogue-community; and did so with much rhetorical power. In fact, these words were so rousing that two full decades later, in Cincinnati, Ohio and Easton, Pennsylvania, Jews who were similarly breaking away from established synagogue communities borrowed the identical wording employed here to justify their actions (without giving crediting to the original authors). [29] The shared language demonstrates that in this period there was a nationwide movement to transform and revitalize American Judaism, and that changes and developments in larger communities influenced those in smaller ones.

In Charleston, a more famous schism within the Jewish community took place. Just as it had in New York, the challenge to the synagogue-community came initially from young Jews – whose average age was about thirty-two, while the average age of the leaders of Charleston's Beth Elohim congregation was close to sixty-two.[30] Dissatisfied with "the apathy and neglect which have been manifested towards our holy religion," these young people were also somewhat influenced by the spread of Unitarianism in Charleston, and fearful of Christian missionary activities that had begun to be directed toward local Jews. Above all, like their New York counterparts, they were passionately concerned about Jewish survival ("the future welfare and respectability of the nation"). These concerns led these young people, like their New York counterparts, to petition congregational leaders to break with tradition and institute change.[31] The Charleston reformers were largely native born – their city, mired in an economic downturn, did not attract many immigrants – and the changes in traditional Jewish practice that they sought were far more radical than anything called for in New York. Among other things, they called for an abbreviated service, vernacular prayers, a weekly sermon,

Beth Elohim synagogue, Charleston, SC. Solomon Nunes Carvalho, artist

American Jewish Historical Society

and an end to traditional free will offerings in the synagogue. When, early in 1825, their petition was dismissed out of hand, they, preceding the New Yorkers by several months, created an independent Jewish religious society called The Reformed Society of Israelites for Promoting True Principles of Judaism According to its Purity and Spirit. A fundamental aim of the new society was to replace "blind observance of the ceremonial law" with "true piety… the first great object of our Holy Religion."[32]

Fundamentally, the strategies that were proposed for revitalizing American Judaism in New York differed from those in Charleston. The New Yorkers, influenced by contemporary revivalism, worked within the framework of Jewish law, stressing education and changes in the organization and aesthetics of Jewish religious life. The Charlestonites, on the other hand, were influenced by Unitarianism, and believed that Judaism needed to be reformed in order to bring Jews back to the synagogue. The New Yorkers adumbrated Modern Orthodox Judaism; the Charlestonites Reform Judaism. Both explicitly rejected the traditionalist strategy of the "established" Sephardic congregations. But the issue was more than just strategic. Both secessions challenged the authority of the synagogue community, insisting that America recognized their right to withdraw and worship as they saw fit. In the early decades of the 19th century, Protestants all over the United States were abandoning denominations in which they had been raised. They turned, instead, to those they felt were more democratic, inspiring and authentic; moving, for example, from Congregational, Presbyterian and Episcopal churches to those of the Methodists, Baptists and Disciples of Christ.[33] Jews now followed the same pattern.

Henceforward, in larger communities, dissenters no longer sought to compromise their principles for the sake of consensus. Instead, they felt free to withdraw and start their own synagogues, which they did time and again. In New York, there were two synagogues in 1825, four in 1835, ten in 1845, and more than twenty in 1855. By the Civil War, every major American Jewish community had at least two synagogues, and larger ones like Philadelphia, Baltimore or Cincinnati had four or more. These were not satellite congregations created to meet the needs of dispersed or immigrant Jews, nor were they congregations sanctioned by any central Jewish authority. While in Western Europe church and synagogue hierarchies persisted, in free and democratic America, congregational autonomy largely became the rule – in Judaism as well as in Protestantism. Indeed, new congregations arose largely through a replication of the divisive process that had created B'nai Jeshurun and the Reformed Society of Israelites. Members dissatisfied with their home congregations resigned and created new ones more suited to their needs and desires. Some hard-to-please Jews founded several synagogues in succession.[34]

The result was nothing less than a new American Judaism – a Judaism that was diverse and pluralistic where before it had been designedly monolithic. For the first time, American Jews could now choose from a number of congregations, most of them Ashkenazic in one form or another, reflecting a range of different rites, ideologies, and regions of origin. Inevitably, these synagogues competed with one another for members and for status. As a result they had a new interest in minimizing dissent and keeping members satisfied. Indeed, more than anyone realized at the time, synagogue pluralism changed the balance of power between the synagogue and its members. Before, when there was only one synagogue in every community, that synagogue could take members for granted and discipline them; members had little option but to obey. Now, American Jews did have an option; in fact, synagogues needed them more than they needed any particular synagogue. This led to the rapid demise of the system of disciplining congregants with fines and sanctions. Congregations became much more concerned with attracting members than with keeping them in line.[35]

One final implication of synagogue pluralism: it brought to an end the intimate coupling of synagogue and community. Into the twentieth century the bylaws of Shearith Israel, (today the Spanish and Portuguese Synagogue) still demanded that "all and every person or persons who shall have been considered of the Jewish persuasion, resident within the limits of the Corporation of the City of New York… shall be assessed and charged by the Board of Trustees ten dollars per annum."[36] But the breakdown of the synagogue-community meant that there was no incentive for anyone to pay. Instead, in every major city where Jews lived, the synagogue-community was replaced by a community of synagogues. A single synagogue was no longer able to represent the community as a whole. In fact, synagogues increasingly came to represent *diversity* in American Jewish life – they symbolized and promoted fragmentation. To bind the Jewish community together and carry out functions that the now privatized and functionally delimited synagogues could no longer handle required new community-wide organizations

The result was nothing less than a new American Judaism – a Judaism that was diverse and pluralistic where before it had been designedly monolithic. For the first time, American Jews could now choose from a number of congregations.

that were capable of transcending religious differences. Charitable organizations like the Hebrew Benevolent Society and fraternal organizations like B'nai B'rith soon moved in to fill the void.

By the 1840s, the structure of the American Jewish community mirrored the federalist pattern of the nation as a whole, balanced precariously between unity and diversity. American Judaism had likewise come to resemble the American religious pattern. Jews, many of whom were young, dissatisfied with the American Jewish "establishment," influenced by the world around them, and fearful that Judaism would not continue unless it changed had produced a religious revolution. This revolution overthrew the synagogue communities and replaced a monolithic Judaism with one that was much more democratic, free, diverse, and competitive. American Judaism, as we know it, was shaped by this revolution, and its impact and implications continue to reverberate.

Notes

1. *American Jewish Archives* 7 (January 1955), 51.

2. *Publications of the American Jewish Historical Society* 18 (1909), 4, 5, 20.

3. *Ibid*, 8-37.

4. *American Jewish Archives* 7 (January 1955), 17-23, 56.

5. Morris U. Schappes, *A Documentary History of the Jews in the United States 1654-1875* (New York: Schocken Books, 1971), 19.

6. Jacob R. Marcus, *The Colonial American Jew 1492-1776* (Detroit: Wayne State University Press, 1970), 351.

7. Malcolm H. Stern, "The Sheftall Diaries: Vital Records of Savannah Jewry (1733-1808)," *American Jewish Historical Quarterly* 54 (March 1965), 247.

8. Malcolm H. Stern, "New Light on the Jewish Settlement of Savannah," *American Jewish Historical Quarterly* 52 (1963), 163-199.

9. Lionel D. Barnett (ed. & transl), *El Libro de Los Acuerdos* (Oxford: Oxford University Press, 1931), 3.

10. *Publications of the American Jewish Historical Society* 21 (1913), 50-51.

11. Jacob R. Marcus, *American Jewry-Documents-Eighteenth Century* (Cincinnati: Hebrew Union College Press, 1959), 178.

12. John B. Kirby, "Early American Politics -- The Search for Ideology: An Historiographical Analysis and Critique of the Concept of Deference," *Journal of Politics* 32 (1970), 808-838; J.A.Pocock, "The Classical Theory of Deference," *American Historical Review* 81 (1976), 516-523.

13. Marcus, *American Jewry-Documents-Eighteenth Century*, 149, 150, 154-155.

14. *Ibid*, 155.

15. *Ibid*, 145-146.

16. Daniel J. Elazar, Jonathan D. Sarna and Rela G. Monson (eds.), *A Double Bond: The Constitutional Documents of American Jewry* (Lanham, MD: University Press of America, 1992), 113.

17. Nathan O. Hatch, *The Democratization of American Christianity* (New Haven: Yale University Press, 1989), 6, 64.

18. Samuel Oppenheim, "The Question of the Kosher Meat Supply in New York in 1813: With a Sketch of Earlier Conditions," *Publications of the American Jewish Historical Society* 25 (1917), 54-57; David and Tamar De Sola Pool, *An Old Faith in the New World: Portrait of Shearith Israel 1654-1954* (New York: Columbia University Press, 1955), 243-247.

19. Elazar, Sarna, and Monson, *A Double Bond*, 116.

20. Malcolm H. Stern, "The 1820s: American Jewry Comes of Age," in *A Bicentennial Festschrift for Jacob Rader Marcus*, ed. Bertram W. Korn (New York: Ktav, 1976), 539-549.

21. Haym M. Salomon to Zalegman Phillips (November 30, 1825) in *The Jews of the United States 1790-1840: A Documentary History*, ed. Joseph L. Blau and Salo W. Baron (New York: Columbia University Press, 1963), 547-548.

22. Blau and Baron, *Jews of the United States*, 541.

23. Pool, *An Old Faith in the New World*, 436; cf. Hyman B. Grinstein, *The Rise of the Jewish Community of New York 1654-1860* (Philadelphia: Jewish Publication Society, 1945), 40-49.

24. [New York] *National Advocate*, December 5, 1825, p.2

25. Blau and Baron, *Jews of the United States*, 542-545; see *Christian Inquirer*, September 17, 1825, p.151.

26. Pool, *An Old Faith in the New World*, 437.

27. Israel Goldstein, *A Century of Judaism in New York: B'nai Jeshurun 1825-1925* (New York: B'nai Jeshurun, 1930), 54-55; the original spelling of the congregation's name was "B'nai Yeshiorun."

28. *Ibid*, 55-56.

29. See James G. Heller, *As Yesterday When It Is Past: A History of the Isaac M. Wise Temple…* (Cincinnati: Isaac M. Wise Temple, 1942), 26-27; Joshua Trachtenberg, *Consider the Years: The Story of the Jewish Community of Easton, 1752-1942* (Easton: Temple Brith Sholom, 1944), 237.

30. These average ages are based on incomplete data assembled by Solomon Breibart; see Robert Liberles, "Conflict over Reforms: The Case of Congregation Beth Elohim, Charleston, South Carolina," in Jack Wertheimer (ed.), *The American Synagogue: A Sanctuary Transformed* (New York: Cambridge University Press, 1987), 282.

31. L.C.Moise, *Biography of Isaac Harby* (Charleston: n.p., 1931); Lou H. Silberman, *American Impact: Judaism in the United States in the Early Nineteenth Century* The B.G. Rudolph Lectures in Judaic Studies (Syracuse: Syracuse University, 1964); James W. Hagy, *This Happy Land: The Jews of Colonial and Antebellum Charleston* (Tuscaloosa: University of Alabama Press, 1993), 128-160; Gary Phillip Zola, *Isaac Harby of Charleston, 1788-1828* (Tuscaloosa: University of Alabama Press, 1994), 112-149.

32. Moise, *Biography of Isaac Harby*, 61.

33. Hatch, *The Democratization of American Christianity*, 59.

34. Grinstein, *Rise of the Jewish Community of New York*, 472-474; Gerard R. Wolfe, *The Synagogues of New York's Lower East Side* (New York: New York University Press, 1978), 37.

35. Jonathan D. Sarna, "The Evolution of the American Synagogue," in Robert M. Seltzer and Norman J. Cohen (eds.), *The Americanization of the Jews* (New York: NYU Press, 1995), 219-221.

36. Pool, *An Old Faith in the New World*, 264.

Pioneering: Jewish Men and Women of the American West

William Toll

By the 1870s, the
Jewish merchant with a
brick store and growing
family was just as
authentic a symbol of
western settlement as
were the wagon train,
the mining camp, and
the cavalry.

Pioneering and the Revitalization of Identity

After the California Gold Rush, Jewish men and women in the American West forged new identities as pioneers of a new society. Nevertheless, they retained intimate contact with a cosmopolitan Jewish world. Beginning as European villagers beset by medieval restrictions, young brothers, usually with family assistance, immigrated into the vast expanse of the American nation. But even as bachelors they created benevolent societies and synagogues to meet economic, social and ritual needs, and after marriage their young wives created female benevolent societies to assist one another with child rearing and charity. By the 1870s, the Jewish merchant with a brick store and growing family was just as authentic a symbol of western settlement as were the wagon train, the mining camp, and the cavalry. In an unflattering gloss, John G. Bourke in 1881 described the streets of Sante Fe as "filled by day with a motley crew of hook-nosed Jews, blue-coated soldiers, and señoritas wrapped to the eyes in *rebosos*." [1]

Pioneering Jews identified themselves as members of a sophisticated merchant class. Most of these merchants, in cities all over the country, supported a new American Judaism that combined more personalized religiosity with an elite sense of public responsibility.[2] By the 1890s, business alliances, modern ideas about family nurturing and philanthropy, and new religious institutions served to reconnect Jewish women and men of the West with Jews in other parts of the New World.[3] But the high civic status of Jews in remote locales gave them a distinctive, regional sense of pride, a feeling quite opposite from the anxieties felt by their colleagues in Germany and France.[4] In the small towns of the West, Jewish merchants and their families were prominent citizens. In Los Angeles in 1876, the parade honoring the nation's centennial was led by a young Jewish girl, Carrie Cohn, who portrayed the Goddess of Liberty. The city's formal ceremonies ended with a benediction from Rabbi Abraham Edelman of Congregation B'nai B'rith.[5] In Trinidad, Colorado, a predominantly Hispanic mining town of 5,500 in 1890, Solomon and Sam Jaffa of the Jaffa Mercantile Company had built the local opera house. By the late 1880s, the British liberal Norman Angell described the Weil brothers of Bakersfield, California as "the type of Jew who represented at the time in the new country the most cultured and civilized element in the community." [6]

Central European Setting

Young Jews came to the West in the 1850s because they were caught in the tumultuous economic, political and cultural upheavals that engulfed Central Europe. Agricultural society in the German states had for some time been organized by a landed nobility, worked by a peasant majority, and sanctified by state-supported churches. Jews, living in small villages, peddled through the countryside or served as middlemen in the grain and cattle trades. By the mid-19th century, however, a new economic system based on the enclosure of agricultural land, railroad transportation, and rudimentary textile and iron factories, had induced the massive migration of rural people and made the local peddler obsolete. A freer flow of ideas challenged the authority of religious conservatives. In the face of a fragmenting social structure, German state governments fostered cultural integration through a policy of *bildung,* or cultural "improvement." To the Jews, *bildung* promised political equality and access to state employment should they acquire the German language and secular culture. By the 1840s, most Jewish boys in Bavaria or Hesse continued to apprentice with male relatives as merchants or artisans, but they had abandoned the *chedarim* and *yeshivot* for a secular education in government-supported gymnasia.[7] Knowledge of the wider world as well as traditional artisan skills were thought to be useful, because fathers were convinced that they and their sons would have to earn a living elsewhere.[8]

The Ehrman brothers and their wives displayed the elite sensibilities of prosperous western Jews. Portland, 1892

Jewish Historical Society of Oregon

While no studies exist of the relocation of Jewish heads of families to German cities, most Jewish young men did migrate in search of work. By the mid-19th century, brothers followed one another out of the "dorfs" and "burgs," until Jews became the most urbanized religious community in the newly unified Germany, as well as in Austria and Hungary. Jews now married at a later age. They had far fewer children than their parents had, and far fewer than equivalent Christian middle class families.[9] By the 1890s, sons were attending universities, entering the "free" professions like law, and, to a lesser extent, joining the civil service. Daughters acquired the domestic skills appropriate to merchant families, and were often tutored in modern languages.[10]

Despite new access to education and employment, cultural alienation and political proscription continued to plague urbanized European Jewry. Although Jews acquired more wealth and education and became more acculturated to German secular values,[11] the requirements for entering the new middle class (*Bildungsburgertum*) seemed more difficult to meet. European academics, though promoting a "scientific" study of society that claimed to be "value free," still stigmatized Judaism as morally archaic. Artisans and peasants continued to believe that the Talmud justified the exploitation of Christians by pawnbrokers and moneylenders. Even in the most cosmopolitan of cities, strident political anti-Semitism denied Jews a feeling of authentic citizenship. In capitals like Vienna, Berlin and Paris, anti-Semitic political parties vied for office by blaming the "alien Jew" for the displacement of artisans and shopkeepers.[12] Far more frequently than ever before, Jewish young people were marrying gentiles and converting to Protestant Christianity to escape stigma and to enhance their social status.

Jaffa Mercantile Company, Trinidad, CO, ca. 1870

American Jewish Archives

Immigration

Between 1840 and 1873, more than two and a half million Germans immigrated to America. The two hundred thousand Jews among them represented a far greater proportion than their numbers in the German population.[13] Jewish boys in their early teens boarded the new steamships at Bremen, Hamburg or Rotterdam to apprentice with relatives who had preceded them to New York. As Bernice Degginger Greengard of Seattle recalled, her paternal grandfather, Simon Degginger, left the little town of Degginin near Stuttgart to evade the draft. "My father's father came alone to America when he was sixteen. He stayed in New York… learning the language, and was apprenticed to a painter." Bernhard Goldsmith, later mayor of Portland, Oregon, recalled that in 1848 at age sixteen, he left Weddenburg, near Munich, for New York to apprentice as a watchmaker with a cousin. As the oldest son in a large, mercantile family, Bernhard thought that economic opportunities were shrinking in Bavaria, and that his responsibility was to find new ones.[14] Some young Jews peddled among the farm families from New England and Germany that were relocating along the new road networks and canals that extended from New York to Illinois.[15] Other Jewish peddlers went south to Memphis, New Orleans and later to Atlanta.

Mayor Bernhard Goldsmith of Portland, Oregon

Jewish Historical Society of Oregon

The Gold Rush lured thousands of young men to the Pacific Coast, where they utilized ancestral trading skills to reach remote ranches and mining camps. One of the most successful, Lewis Gerstle of San Francisco, whose Alaska Commercial Company controlled the fur trade in the 1870s and 1880s, even returned to Germany to retrace the route over which his father had peddled as a boy.[16] When Jews acquired sufficient capital to become sedentary merchants, they sent younger brothers or cousins to take their place managing small general stores in remote towns. In the 1880s, Ben Selling of Portland wrote to a prospective colleague about opportunities. "I know two or three places in eastern Oregon where you can do good business and make several thousand a year. All our

merchants who have any business capacity are doing well; only those do not
succeed who have no ideas of business, having been farmers or sheepmen all their
lives."[17] As late as 1910, Herman Wertheim, through the intercession of his older
brother, arrived in Bernalillo, New Mexico. He was one of many young men to
clerk and then operate a store for the Seligman brothers in an even more remote
town. "This is how the German-Jewish boys got their start in business,"
Wertheim recalled.[18]

In cities like San Francisco and Portland, Jewish merchants usually
persisted longer than most other residents, in part because they owned property
but also because their wives refused to remain in remote towns for too long.
Julius Durkheimer was born in Philadelphia in 1857, and was brought to Portland,
Oregon by his parents, Bavarian immigrants, just after the Civil War. In 1888,
he opened his own store in Baker, Oregon, a railhead for the Union Pacific,
and sent his three younger brothers to manage branches in Burns and in Canyon
City. But Durkheimer's son Sylvan recalled learning that when
Julius married Delia Fried in 1889, he had to promise her that
they would stay in eastern Oregon only until he had earned
enough money to resettle the family in a larger city. By 1896
the Durkheimers returned to Portland, where Julius bought
into a large wholesale produce business.[19]

The class structure of the
western United States
was only beginning to
coalesce, so that Jews,
rather than being
perceived as abettors in
the destruction of an old
social order, became
partners in the creation
of a new one.

Charles Strauss and son

Arizona Historical Society

Jewish immigrants to the West started business
ventures similar to those of their cousins who were migrating
to the cities of Central Europe. But the very different political
cultures led to very different civic positions. The class
structure of the western United States was only beginning to
coalesce, so that Jews, rather than being perceived as abettors
in the destruction of an old social order, became partners in
the creation of a new one. When men like Bernard Goldsmith
or Julius Durkheimer served in militias, volunteer fire
companies, and on school boards, and held the office of mayor,
they did so not as spokesmen for a stigmatized group, but as
citizens defending life, liberty, and property. Because
so many Jews participated prominently in public life, they
cemented their community to the forces that upheld law and
order. Narrow-shouldered, bespectacled Charles Strauss, mayor
of Tucson in the 1880s, was typical of civically-active frontier
Jews. An extraordinary photograph shows him looking soberly
at the camera with a shot gun in his left hand, a gun belt
studded with bullets around his waist, and a cigar dangling
between the index and middle fingers of his right hand.
His son, similarly armed and attired, but without the cigar,
stands beside him. This immigrant from a Bavarian village initiated the building of
Tucson's city hall, fire station and library and created its first building and loan
association. Had he moved to Munich or remained in New York he could never
have been addressed as "Mr. Mayor."

Several examples illustrate the scope of entrepreneurial operations and its
relationship both to family mobility and civic politics. In the 1870s, young Aaron
Meier started a general store in Portland, which was overshadowed both by
importing houses that specialized in dry goods and glassware and by other general
stores. With the aid of a younger partner, Sigmund Frank, he peddled among local
farmers (whose produce was sold in the store's basement), with prostitutes who
always paid cash for their linens, and with thousands of Chinese laborers who lived
in the nearby rooming house district. In the 1890s his wife, Jeanette Hirsch (the
power behind the business), brought her younger brothers from Germany to work

in the store. Then, the Hirsch brothers went to apprentice at the John Wanamaker store in Philadelphia, where they learned about innovative retailing and "set pricing." By the early 20th century, with their help, Meier & Frank had grown into the largest department store in the Pacific Northwest. It was housed in Portland's most impressive commercial building and had more influence over downtown real estate than any local business except the banks. The Hirsch brothers, however, were growing restive under their sister Jeanette's authority, and in 1907 they broke away to manufacture crude waterproof garments for loggers. Over the next thirty years the Hirsch brothers and their sons, under the trade name "White Stag," created a new industry of all-weather clothing that set styling standards. Their logo, emblazoned on a huge neon sign, became a virtual symbol of the city.[20]

Adolph Sutro, a far more intense and imaginative personality, arrived in America from Bavaria in 1850 at age twenty, accompanying his widowed mother and nine siblings. His older brother and mother opened a general store in

Like many Jewish businessmen, Santa Fe retailer Charles Ilfeld followed a brother to New Mexico. Ilfeld carried on his business correspondence from this monumental walnut patent desk.

Palace of the Governors collection, Museum of New Mexico

Baltimore, but Adolph came to Stockton, California, where he joined a cousin in a general store that supplied miners. After the discovery of the Comstock Silver Lode in Nevada Territory in 1860, he and a brother opened a refining mill in Virginia City. After a good deal of study and extraordinary political manipulation, including the negotiation of a charter from the United States Congress in 1866 and financial support from the miners, he built the Sutro Tunnel to improve the efficiency and safety of the operations. He invested his profits in San Francisco, where he developed large tracts of real estate and gained fame as the builder of elaborate public baths. His flamboyant personality and respect for miners and artisans made him a political spokesman for skilled, unionized workers, who supported his successful mayoral candidacy in the mid-1890s.[21]

Far more exploitative and atypical of Jewish "pioneers" were the Guggenheim brothers, who went west not to settle, but to expand the family fortune. Their father, Meyer, emigrated from a Swiss village to Philadelphia in the late 1830s, and while peddling in the Pennsylvania countryside he studied the unfilled household needs of his customers. He concocted a better formula for stove polish, learned to mix cheap coffee substitutes, and, on the advice of a cousin, bought a factory in Switzerland to manufacture inexpensive lace. By the late 1870s, Meyer was apprenticing his sons in various segments of the family empire, when a former gentile business associate from Philadelphia persuaded him to buy into two silver mines in Leadville, Colorado. Meyer and two of his sons soon learned that much of the wealth in mining was derived from smelting rather than extracting the ores. Negotiating land and tax concessions from the pliant city council of Pueblo, Colorado, they opened a massive smelter in the 1880s. In the 1890s they, like the Rockefellers, expanded their mining and smelting operations into Mexico. Although the Colorado legislature elected Simon Guggenheim to the United States Senate in 1906, the center of the family's social and philanthropic life remained New York. Their "absentee ownership" and indifference to the welfare of miners made them much-hated "robber barons."[22]

The Outsider as Insider

By asserting themselves as civic partners, Jews of the West also established who they were not. Traditional anti-Semitism had rested on the stigma of "the other," of the threateningly primitive or the subversive. But in the American West, this stigma fell on peoples who had not inhabited Europe. The native peoples who managed to survive diseases were being "subdued" by the United States army as the remnants of "savagery." The Sioux and Cheyenne warriors of the plains and the Apache in the Southwest symbolized the resistance of vast spaces to the Europeans' struggle to husband and harvest God's domain.[23] Chinese immigrants as early as the 1850s were stigmatized as Godless "heathen," interloping on the expansion of Western civilization and the competition for surface gold. While their labor was exploited in the construction of railroads and levees, federal legislation denied them naturalized citizenship.[24] By the 1870s, the Chinese were the focus

Solomon Bibo at the Acoma Pueblo, 1883

Museum of New Mexico Neg. no. 16049

of the West's "race problem," investigated by legislatures, discriminated against in law, and intensively segregated in cities like San Francisco and Portland.[25]

As an organized community Jews generally did not defend the abstract rights of more severely stigmatized groups. However, they rarely saw themselves as conquerors of "savages," though Sutro in Nevada and Michael Goldwater in Arizona applied the term to bands that attacked their supply wagons. Jews traded on the edges of reservations and acted as interpreters. Solomon Bibo, one of three brothers trading in New Mexico, married the Native American granddaughter of the governor of the Acoma Pueblo in 1885, and was himself appointed governor in 1888. Nor did Jews envision a "Yellow Peril" against which they needed legal or economic defense. Instead, merchants and owners of small factories employed Chinese as servants and as mill hands. In 1873 in Portland, Mayor Philip Wasserman vetoed an ordinance that prohibited Chinese from being hired on municipal construction projects, because he believed it violated federal treaties.[26] In 1879 in San Francisco and in 1886 in Portland, Jews upheld civic authority by joining posses to protect Chinese rooming houses from attacks by vigilante mobs. As Ben Selling wrote to a cousin,

> We have been threatened with serious trouble on account of the Chinese agitation. At Oregon City the Anti-Coolie Club drove the Chinamen out of town during the night. The better class of citizens deprecate this and here in Portland have enrolled about two hundred deputy sheriffs. I am one and have done patrol duty two nights… I think the organization of citizens will prevent any riot, but if there is one, somebody is going to get hurt.[27]

Jewish settlers were mainly absorbed in gaining security for their families, but occasionally they had to use their mercantile stature to ward off anti-Semitic gestures. In Portland in 1886, Ben Selling organized Jewish storekeepers throughout the state to oppose the election of a Judge Waldo to the state supreme court. Selling described Waldo as a "bitter Jew-hater" and reported that Waldo had said he "never knew a Jew to come into court with a straight case." Because Selling

By asserting themselves as civic partners, Jews of the West also established who they were not. Traditional anti-Semitism had rested on the stigma of "the other," of the threateningly primitive or the subversive. But in the American West, this stigma fell on peoples who had not inhabited Europe.

felt that suspicion of Jews was widespread, he advised his colleagues not to mention anti-Semitism, but to emphasize instead Waldo's general unfitness for the judicial post. "To make a public race fight would insure his election as there are many Jew-haters in Oregon," Selling concluded.[28]

Western Pioneers as Ritual Jews

As they entered the secular society of 19th century Europe and the United States, Jews redefined Judaism. Whereas it had been a sacred law defining their activities, it was now considered a mere religion based on tenets of faith. As citizens of the Jewish faith, Jews could survive as equals in religiously "plural" societies. Rabbis attracted to the idea of "Reform" abandoned the binding authority of Jewish law (*halacha*), and concepts like exile (*galut*) and a return (*yishuv*) to Zion. To replace them, they adopted a creed that came to include a "mission of Israel" for moral reform. Their refurbished ritual, without caps or prayer shawls, but with choirs, organs, and sermons, reconciled their new "identity" as citizens with a residue of faith in being "chosen" for a unique destiny. Rabbis and urban intellectuals debated the new meaning of Judaism – of what it meant to be "chosen" – in liberalized societies that at least putatively defined them as equal citizens.[29]

Businessmen in the towns of the American West were not educated to dispute theological issues. Instead, they reproduced a few basic rituals that fulfilled their moral obligations. Their synagogues held brief services on Sabbath eve and on High Holy Days, and they insisted on ritual burial in Jewish holy ground. After they had families, they also insisted on circumcision of newborn males and the holding of Passover Seders. Where possible they hired rabbis to hold lengthier Saturday morning services and to initiate Sunday schools. But before starting families, these congregations – comprised of the generation born and educated in the American West – generally rejected rabbis who insisted on systematic reform. Nevertheless, the regularity of Jewish ritual, as well as the occasional elegance of new temples like Emanu-el in San Francisco, made Jewish observance a moral support of the new cosmopolitan social order.[30]

The fulfillment of ritual obligations caught young Jews in cultural crosscurrents that fostered civic participation. The absence of ordained rabbis gave these young men and women – businessmen, clerks and artisans – the opportunity to engage in the symbolic maintenance of moral continuity. By creating a *minyan*, by obtaining a charter for a cemetery, and by building a synagogue, they demonstrated to the wider society how a religious community that was usually perceived as marginal reconstituted itself to combat the anarchic forces of sinfulness and savagery. Although religious ceremonies were generally rudimentary and poorly attended, early synagogue buildings were often the site for secular education and the meeting room for male and female benevolent societies, while the trustees maintained the public space of a cemetery. Jewish women, by recreating the home-centered rituals of traditional Judaism, fulfilled the new middle class expectation that mothers infuse the home with a spiritual aura.

Protestant philanthropy in small towns throughout the West supported missionary churches, which maintained tract and temperance societies, struggled to promote bible reading, and attempted to abolish saloons and brothels. Most Protestant ministers sent west by Presbyterian, Congregational, and Episcopalian philanthropy saw the Jewish merchants and their religious institutions, whatever the stereotypes about them as "Hebrews," as quiet allies in establishing a morally sound community.[31] As contributors to the culture of reform, rabbis like Jacob Voorsanger of San Francisco and younger rabbis like William Friedman of Denver and Stephen Wise of Portland exchanged pulpits with liberal Protestant ministers,

> Businessmen in the towns of the American West were not educated to dispute theological issues. Instead, they reproduced a few basic rituals that fulfilled their moral obligations.

and led crusades to curtail gambling, end prostitution, and cleanse politics of "corruption."[32]

Jews who created institutions like the regional orphanage in San Francisco, hospitals for tubercular patients in Denver and in Los Angeles, or who initiated the visiting nurse service in Seattle added to the whole city's philanthropic infrastructure. Commissioning architectural landmarks added to the prestige of the Jewish elite, especially in San Francisco, where mercantile families like the Sterns, the Fleishackers, the Brandensteins, and the Haases contributed a civic grove, and provided endowments for a zoo, the opera, the symphony, and an art museum. In 19th century Germany, wealthy Jews contributed heavily to civic philanthropy primarily to demonstrate their fitness for inclusion in the new bourgeois elite.[33] In cities of the West, however, they worked with the Protestant elite to bring culture to rustic landscapes, and they were perceived as men and women whose communal presence symbolized the refined edge of cultural conquest.

Like the Protestant churches and Masonic lodges, Jewish communal institutions sanctified a network on which ethnic self-reliance rested. For mutual benefit services, men formed local Hebrew Benevolent Societies, and then lodges of the national fraternal order of B'nai B'rith. The initial functions of benevolent societies were to provide members with "insurance" in case of sickness and to guarantee them ritual burial. As was true of the mutual benefit societies for many immigrant groups, The Hebrew Benevolent Societies also established small pools of capital to lend interest-free to members trying to start businesses. As more money accumulated, sums were lent to non-Jews, usually for mortgages, at prevailing rates of interest to generate more capital for members or to be used for philanthropic purposes.

Young men usually started B'nai B'rith lodges for similar mutual benefit services, and also for the opportunity to participate in the cosmopolitan Jewish world. As Jonathan Woocher noted, B'nai B'rith's network of lodges provided a secular agenda for a Jewish identity now grounded in participation as civic equals.[34] At the national level, B'nai B'rith orchestrated secular Jewish activism by lobbying the United States government to intervene against anti-Semitic assaults in Europe. Locally, city directories always listed B'nai B'rith lodges with their officers and meeting times so that the "Hebrew" pioneers could be collectively identified as civic equals.

By the 1890s, changes in the activities and focus of lodges reflected a major shift in gender relations in the Jewish community. Earlier, the lodges had provided a place of relaxation for bachelors and young married men accustomed to a world clearly divided into male and female spheres. At meetings, much of what had been discussed was the health and welfare of members, as well as campaigns of importance to the national office. Now, however, the meetings were divided into business and social segments, and fiancées and wives were invited to the latter. Indeed, wives and fiancées often provided musical entertainment, such as piano and violin recitals, and the singing of semi-classical arias. Portland's B'nai B'rith Lodge 416 even hired professionals for musical entertainment.[35]

The acceptance of diversity within the merchant class encouraged young Jewish store owners and clerks in the 1880s to create their own social clubs, just as young Protestant merchants were doing. When, in the early 1890s, business leaders in San Francisco and Portland emulated their counterparts in large East Coast cities by initiating a directory of "elite families," the entire membership list of the Jewish social club "Concordia" was included. Indeed, because of the high social status of Jewish pioneer families,

Like the Protestant churches and Masonic lodges, Jewish communal institutions sanctified a network on which ethnic self-reliance rested.

far more Jewish families were included in these elite "blue books" than the proportion of Jews in the local population. The Concordia clubhouse became a center for upper middle-class acculturation with its facilities for card-playing and other "gentlemanly" functions, as well as a large ballroom. And like the new B'nai B'rith lodges, Concordia responded to a greater sense of shared experience between men and women by sponsoring costume balls, formal dances and dinners for members and their wives.

Masonic lodges, which identified local business and professional elites, welcomed prominent Jewish merchants and lawyers, many of whom were elected as officers. As an ideology, Freemasonry provided a non-evangelical, Judaeo-Christian vehicle for self-made men to venerate the ethical achievements of the Old Testament patriarchs, especially Moses the lawgiver, and Solomon, who hired the masons to construct God's Holy Temple. Central to Masonry's initiatory rite was a belief in Solomon's ability to extract from the slain master-architect of the Temple the plans for its completion. Jews selected for membership in Masonic lodges could, in an elite ecumenical setting, express faith in their own Biblical heroes while not having to mention Jesus. When Alex Sinsheimer was elected Grand Master of the Oregon Odd Fellows in 1886, his older business partner, Ben Selling, congratulated him. "You may feel proud to win such a distinction at your early age and it is a double honor since you are one of the proscribed race." [36]

Gender and Generation

The lives of Jewish women in America between the 1850s and 1890s changed perhaps even more than did the lives of men, as they bore children and created families thousands of miles from their home towns. Most Jewish women entered the West through the institution of marriage, but some unmarried young women had immigrated to America to join relatives in regional marketing centers like St. Louis and San Francisco, where they became part of the "marriage pool." [37] Others, at least through the early 1870s, were married in Germany to men who had returned from America specifically to find a bride. Once they arrived in the American West, young wives had to create a network of nurture because they lacked the daily assistance of mothers and sisters and of a state-supported Jewish community.

As young women now relocated to remote towns, they repeated many traditional family patterns. Usually, in their late teens or early twenties, they married men at least ten years older than themselves, who expected them to oversee a large, patriarchal household. They became pregnant almost immediately after marriage and over fifteen years usually had six to ten children, around whom they created a social life. As wives of merchants, they almost never held jobs outside the home. They could expect to have a servant girl, and perhaps two or three if their husbands had built large businesses. As late as 1880 their unmarried daughters rarely held formal employment, but were listed in the federal manuscript census as "at home."

Indeed the home itself might be more properly thought of as a flexible household. The members often spanned two or three generations and included not only the husband and wife but also several of their unmarried adult brothers and sisters. For example, Sylvan Durkheimer explained that if an older couple had a married daughter or son,

...then this [younger] couple moved in to maintain house for the elderly couple. My parents did the same thing when they moved here to Portland from Burns. They moved in with my mother's parents and two bachelor

Once they arrived in the American West, young wives had to create a network of nurture because they lacked the daily assistance of mothers and sisters and of a state-supported Jewish community.

brothers and maintained house for them until the demise of the grandparents. [T]hen my parents moved into their new home on 24th and Lovejoy, [and] these two bachelor brothers moved with them and were regular residents in our family home. [38]

As Paula Hyman has noted, the wives of frontier merchants were expected to sustain a religious aura within the family.[39] While frontier women showed no interest in reintroducing the *mikveh*, or ritual bath, they usually lit Sabbath candles and prepared the home for Passover. Frontier women practiced a modified version of "orthodoxy," and showed no knowledge of the philosophical tenets of "Reform." Yet they expected their daughters as well as their sons to practice Judaism in a fashion commensurate with their new status as successful citizens. Certainly no evidence exists to suggest that in the 19th century immigrant Jews of the West showed any interest in reviving the *cheder*.

"Kosher Picnic,"
National Council of
Jewish Women,
ca. 1895

Beck Archives of Rocky
Mountain Jewish History,
Center for Judaic Studies
and Penrose Library,
University of Denver

Instead, synagogues usually expanded beyond Sabbath and High Holy day services when enough children had reached school age and when the mothers insisted they receive a modicum of instruction. Until then, most religious training occurred in the home. For example, Mrs. Bernice Degginger Greengard in Seattle remembered that at the turn of the 20th century, her mother, who had had no formal religious education, did not keep a kosher kitchen, "but we used to light the candles and my mother taught my brother and myself. In fact, [on Saturday morning] she ran a little Sunday school in her home," which was attended by eight or ten neighborhood children.[40] The Deggingers also observed Chanukah, Purim and of course Passover. Fearful that immigrant girls especially would receive no Jewish education, Mrs. Degginger later organized a Sunday school in Seattle's Jewish settlement house.

Because pioneer husbands and their unmarried male colleagues conducted themselves as a separate social circle, attending Masonic, B'nai B'rith, and Concordia lodge meetings late into the night, as well as serving on the boards of trade and on city councils, the women were expected to create a corresponding set of friendships and social activities. Everywhere, the Ladies' Hebrew Benevolent societies became vehicles for sustaining family life and defining the values on which women's identity should rest. According to the charter in Portland in the 1870s, they were open to "ladies of the Jewish faith," and they were to "administer relief to the poor, the needy and the sick, and to prepare the dead [women and children] for interment." [41] In a small town like

Trinidad, Colorado, where Jews numbered about one hundred and seventy in 1900, the Ladies' Hebrew Benevolent Society not only provided nursing and other support for its members, but through its annual Strawberry Festival created the Jewish communal persona. The festival, membership events like bridge whists, and dues raised funds to furnish the synagogue and even pay its mortgage.[42]

The traditional Biblical ideal of the "woman of valor," sacrificing the "self" for tranquility in the household, elided the Victorian idea of "true womanhood," which required the mistress of the household to create a "haven" of emotional security in a world dominated by ruthless capitalist competition. Leading American Reform rabbis like Kaufman Kohler not only accepted the gendered nostrums of the age, but also grounded them in biological determinants. Kohler, advocating a "mission" for Jews to participate in campaigns for social reform, wrote, "[women's] sympathies are broader and more tender than those of the stern strugglers for existence in the business mart."[43] In San Francisco rabbis like Jacob Voorsanger and Jacob Nieto also wanted American Jewish women to be well-educated and to share some responsibility for administering communal institutions, not because women were equal to men but because of their inherent differences.[44]

The matrons were trained to agree. Alice Gerstle Levison of San Francisco remembered that her wealthy father, Lewis, treated her mother, who was fifteen years younger than he, "like a little girl who had to be protected." Alice found her life equally circumscribed. She and her six siblings even spent two years in Germany in the care of governesses. In San Francisco the round of private schools, tutors and parties exclusively with Jewish friends created a provincial elite that fabricated its own rewards. "Although we were always restricted in some respects," Mrs. Levison recalled, "it was a period in which we were helped to be women and to grow up to meet people."[45] Elsie Stern Haas, who was a generation younger, also remembered how her mother arranged her social life. Though there were by then no extended stays in Germany, she was sent to private schools and her friendships were also confined to young Jews.[46]

Gendered assumptions about human nature required that wealthy women become responsible for other women and their children. As the Seattle Ladies' Hebrew Benevolent Society recorded in its Minute Book in 1896, "The great work of sisterly love and benevolence is constantly carried on in a systematic and discriminating but quiet manner known to the needy recipient... The field of benevolence and charity is properly and virtually woman's."[47] Women needed emotional as well as financial support, because death was always close by. Husbands were usually at least a decade older than their wives, and life expectancy was considerably less than today, so a woman in her late thirties might very well find herself a widow with several children. In addition, infant mortality remained high into the mid-1880s. Though very little attention has been paid to this issue for Jewish communities, data on deaths recorded by the rabbis of Portland, Oregon's Temple Beth Israel show that from 1877 through 1885, almost 43% of the deaths were of children younger than ten years of age. By the 1890s, this figure had dropped to fewer than 10%, but over half the deaths were still of people younger than age sixty, mostly men and women leaving behind a spouse and children.[48]

Several memorial statements entered by the benevolent societies to honor the bereaved or deceased provide a glimpse of the ordeal of a "women of valor." A well documented case of bereavement and maternal self-sacrifice is that of Henrietta Goodman, who was born in Louisiana in 1849 and who in her late teens married an L. Goodman, an immigrant from Bavaria who was sixteen years older than she. The couple arrived in Oregon in 1867, and soon had two daughters. However, by 1873 at age twenty-four, Mrs. Goodman had lost her husband and one of her daughters, for whom Temple Beth Israel had provided the carriage for the funeral and the burial plot. In 1875, Mrs. Goodman left Portland for "a distant part of the country," perhaps

Betty Spiegelberg was only seventeen when she made the journey from Germany to Santa Fe with her new husband, Levi.

Portrait of
Betty Spiegelberg
ca. 1860

Palace of the
Governors Collection
Museum of New Mexico

to return to her native state. So moved by her losses and impressed by her personality were her fellow members of the Benevolent Society that they passed in her honor the only resolution to a living member recorded in their minute books. It read in part, "She was very zealous in the holy cause of charity, and who having undergone many trials and tribulations herself, knew well how to sympathize with the suffering and distress of others."[49] The theme of sacrifice for a broader social good was reiterated all across the West. In 1898 at Trinidad, Colorado, Mrs. Helena Goldsmith was commended for her "words of comfort to all, regardless of creed, color or race… In her unselfish and noble life, she has taught us all that the highest aim in life should and must be to live for others."[50]

By the 1890s, Jewish women, far more than their husbands and brothers, began to supplement frontier self-reliance with more professional standards of public responsibility. In San Francisco during the depression of 1893, Rabbi Voorsanger of Temple Emanu-el suggested that the wives of prominent members emulate several New York synagogues by founding a Sisterhood for Personal Service. The Sisterhood's members were embarrassed at the prospect of immigrant Jews begging in San Francisco as if it were Warsaw, and provided an employment bureau as well as emergency rations for impoverished families. Some of the Sisterhood's younger members also looked to Jane Addams in Chicago and Lillian Wald in New York to learn how educated women addressed complex urban problems. It was decided that classes for poor women would include formal training in ways to prepare a healthful diet, keep a kitchen garden, and sew clothing efficiently. Babies were required to have check-ups at medical clinics and young girls were to be kept out of dance halls and enrolled in clubs. Visiting nurses and female doctors were enlisted to talk to immigrant women about "sex hygiene" and the avoidance of pregnancy. [51]

In the first decade of the 20th century, the new National Council of Jewish Women undertook the effort to "professionalize" the work of the "woman of valor," especially through alliances with public agencies like schools and juvenile courts. Their educated and enlightened perception of gender had little opportunity to flourish in small towns. But in cities like Denver, Portland, Seattle, San Francisco and Los Angeles, the revolution in which women brought professional training to domestic work, and made domestic issues the focus of urban politics was underway. Through settlement work, Jewish women replaced the pioneering ideal of communal self-reliance with a more cosmopolitan ideal that subordinated volunteers to professionals. As a sign of the new integration of local women's social work into national networks, most of the West's first Jewish professional social workers were recruited from New York or Chicago. But these first professionals expected to recruit colleagues from among young Sisterhood volunteers.

The newly sophisticated female intelligence was clearly expressed by the best-educated Jewish woman on the West Coast at the turn of the century, Jessica Peixotto. While completing research for her doctorate on French Socialism at the University of California, she wrote from Lyon in 1896 to a female friend comparing her observations of French women with her own status in America.

> I feel, in my American arrogance, as though I had come here to look upon things as they were, to step into the customs and ideals of a more primitive stage in the 'ascent of man.' When I permit myself this impertinent thought, I smile to think what messieurs of the faculte and all the great ones of the earth would say to such a judgment, they who think of America as a rather outside-the-world sort of place, where all sorts of frantic experiments in radicalism, in mental anarchy and in mere material prosperity are being tried, with none too admirable results. Perhaps it is because I am a woman, and an unmarried one too, that I think this way about la belle France. [52]

Five years later Miss Peixotto tried to bring her views on social reform to her fellow members of the newly established San Francisco section of the Council of Jewish Women. As first head of the section's Philanthropic Committee, she recruited professors from local universities to lecture on the relationship between industrialization and the need for vocational education. To prepare her members she had them read Friedrich Engels' work on housing conditions among the poor of London. At her initiative the section also voted to discuss any topic that could be interpreted as having a bearing on the Jews of San Francisco.[53]

For the associates of Miss Peixotto, the status derived from pioneering implicitly supported reform civic leadership in a setting as cosmopolitan as any other in America. By the turn of the 20th century, American-born Jewish women of the West modernized their communities' philanthropic agendas by linking proliferating social needs to innovative public agencies. The migration from the villages of Central Europe to the new towns and cities of the American frontier, despite a residue of folk prejudice and elite discrimination, had created women as well as men supremely confident of their ability to shape commercial, civic and philanthropic life.

Notes

1. Henry J. Tobias, *A History of the Jews in New Mexico* (Albuquerque, 1990), 56.

2. Charles H. Lippy, *Being Religious, American Style, A History of Popular Religiosity in the United States* (Westport, 1994), 123, 156.

3. Hasia Diner, *A Time for Gathering, The Second Migration, 1820-1880* (Baltimore, 1992), 86. The development of Reform Judaism as a centralized, rationalized system is explained in Alan Silverstein, *Alternatives to Assimilation, The Response of Reform Judaism to American Culture, 1840-1930* (Hanover, NH, 1994), 117-33.

4. See, for example, the "requirements" for Jews in the German states who wished to join the new bourgeoisie, in Shulamit Volkov, "The 'Verburgerliching' of the Jews as a Paradigm," in Jurgen Kocja & Allen Mitchel, eds., *Bourgeois Society in Nineteenth Century Europe* (Oxford/Providence, 1993), 373.

5. Michael E. Engh, S. J., *Frontier Faith, Church, Temple and Synagogue in Los Angeles, 1846-1888* (Albuquerque, 1992), xi.

6. Norman Angell, *After All, the Autobiography of Norman Angell* (London, 1951), 51.

7. See Michael Meyer, *The Origins of the Modern Jew, Jewish Identity and European Culture in Germany, 1749-1824* (Detroit, 1967), 146, 157, 160-66. Meyer notes that rabbis needed degrees from German universities to qualify for ordination.

8. For the upheaval among village Jews in central Europe see Diner, *Time for Gathering*, 1-35.

9. Vicki Caron, *Between France and Germany, The Jews of Alsace-Lorraine, 1871-1918* (Stanford, 1988); Peter Schmidtbauer, "The Household and Household Forms of Viennese Jews, 1857," *Journal of Family History*, 5,4 (Winter, 1980), 379,382; John E. Knodel, *The Decline of Fertility in Germany, 1871-1939* (Princeton, 1974), 108,136-37; Marian Kaplan, *The Making of the Jewish Middle Class, Women, Family and Identity in Imperial Germany* (New York, 1991), 5-6.

10. Paula Hyman, *Gender and Assimilation in Modern Jewish History, The Roles and Representation of Women* (Seattle, 1995), 50-92.

11. Volkov, "The 'Verburgerlichung' of the Jews," 381-2.

12. The literature is very large, but see Michael R. Marrus, *The Politics of Assimilation, A Study of the French Jewish Community at the Time of the Dreyfus Affair* (Oxford, 1971); Ismar Schorsch, *Jewish Reactions to German Anti-Semitism,1870-1914* (New York, 1972); Carl E. Schorske, *Fin-de-Siecle Vienna, Politics and Culture* (New York, 1980)118-29; Peter Gay, "Introduction, German Questions," in Gay, *Freud, Jews and Other Germans* (Oxford & New York, 1978), 3-28.

13. Diner,*Time for Gathering*, 56, summarizes Jewish population growth in the United States, 1820s to 1880. Avraham Barkai, *Branching Out, German Jewish Immigration to the United States, 1820-1914* (New York, 1994), 9-10, estimates that while Jews were about 1.1% of the population of the German states in the 19th century, they were about 4% of the emigrants.

14. "Interview with Bernice Degginger Greengard, (December 6, 1979) 1, Manuscript Collection, University of Washington Libraries; "Bernard Goldsmith," interview, 1-3, November 29, 1889, Hubert Howe Bancroft Collection, Bancroft Library, University of California, Berkeley.

15. Mack Walker, *Germany and the Emigration, 1816-1885* (Cambridge, 1964), 190, says that by the 1870s, German farm families felt that compared to America, rural life in Germany was "wearing down."

16. Mark Lewis Gerstle, "Memories," Bancroft Library; Harriet and Fred Rochlin, *Pioneer Jews, A New Life in the Far West* (Boston, 1984), 130.

17. Ben Selling to B. Scheeline, April 14, 1883, Ben Selling Papers, Oregon Historical Society, Portland, Oregon.

18. Herman Wertheim quoted in Barkai, *Branching Out*, 135.

19. Interview with Sylvan Durkheimer, March 3, 1975, Jewish Historical Society of Oregon.

20. Interview with Harold Hirsch, Jewish Historical Society of Oregon.

21. Robert E. Stewart & Mary F. Stewart, *Adolph Sutro, A Biography* (Berkeley, CA, 1962), 9-33, 47-63.

22. Edwin P. Hoyt, Jr., *The Guggenheims and the American Dream* (New York, 1967), 55 notes in reference to Benjamin Guggenheim, "Like all the Guggenheim sons, he was concerned with becoming an American and a capitalist and was not interested in his Jewishness."

23. The historiography on Native Americans on the Plains is huge. Good introductory, interpretive works are, Robert M. Utley, *The Indian Frontier of the American West, 1846-1890* (Albuquerque, 1984); William T. Hagan, *United States-Comanche Relations, The Reservation Years* (New Haven, 1976); Richard White, *The Roots of Dependency, Subsistence, Environment, and Social Change Among the Choctaws, Pawnees, and Navajo* (Lincoln, 1983).

24. Engh, *Frontier Faiths*, 26.

25. The literature on the Chinese and other Asians is growing. The classic study is Mary Coolidge, *Chinese Immigration* (New York, 1909), and recent scholarly works are Sucheng Chan, *This Bittersweet Soil, The Chinese in California Agriculture*, 1860-1910 (Berkeley, 1986); Sucheng Chan, *Asian Americans, an Interpretive History* (Boston, 1991); Roger Daniels, *Asian Americans, Chinese and Japanese in the United States Since 1859* (Seattle, 1988).

26. E. Kimbark MacColl, *Merchants, Money and Power* (Portland, 1988), 167.

27. Ben Selling to Bennie, March 23, 1886, Selling Papers, Oregon Historical Society.

28. Ben Selling to "Friend Leo", May 21, 1886; Selling to Uncle, May 21, 1886, Ben Selling Papers, Oregon Historical Society.

29. Jonathan Woocher, *Sacred Survival, The Civil Religion of American Jews* (Bloomington, 1986), 8, notes, "[Reform, Neo-Orthodoxy, and the Conservative Movement] shared a fundamental strategy for Jewish survival in the post-Emancipation world; they reconstituted Jewry as a religious group."

30. See Fred Rosenbaum, *Architects of Reform, Congregational and Community Leadership, Emanu-el of San Francisco, 1849-1980* (Berkeley, 1980).

31. The inoffensiveness of the Jews, certainly compared to Irish Catholics, is noted in Robert T. Handy, *Protestant Hopes and Historical Realities* (New York, 1971), 59. The ambivalent image of the Jew is analyzed in Jonathan Sarna, "The 'Mythical Jew' and the Jew Next Door in Nineteenth Century America," in David A. Gerber, ed., *Anti-semitism in American History* (Urbana, 1986), 57-78.

32. Rosenbaum, *Architects of Reform*, 45-65; William Toll, *The Making of an Ethnic Middle Class, Portland Jewry over Four Generations* (Albany, 1982) 97-98.

33. Volkov, "The 'Verburgerlichung'of the Jews," 375; Dolores L. Augustine, "Arriving in the Upper Class; the Wealthy Business Elite of Wilhelmine Germany, in David Blackbourne and Richard J. Evans, eds., *The German Bourgeoisie* (London and New York,1991), 62-63.

34. Woocher, *Sacred Survival*, 22.

35. William Toll, "Fraternalism and Community Structure on the Urban Frontier: The Jews of Portland, Oregon – a Case Study," *Pacific Historical Review*, XLVII, 3 (August 1978), 369-403.

36. Ben Selling to Alex [Sinsheimer], May 21, 1886, Selling Papers, Oregon Historical Society.

37. Diner, *Time for Gathering*, 43, 59.

38. "Sylvan Durkheimer," 6.

39. Hyman, *Gender and Assimilation*, 39-41.

40. Ben Selling to Alex [Sinsheimer], May 21, 1886, Selling Papers, Oregon Historical Society.

41. Toll, *Making Ethnic Middle Class*, 48.

42. Toll, "Domestic Basis of Community," 7; Hoyt, *Guggenheims and American Dream*, 55.

43. "Conference Paper of Dr. K. Kohler," in *Proceedings of the Pittsburgh Rabbinical Conference [1885]* (Richmond, 1923), 10, American Jewish Archives, Cincinnati, Ohio.

44. See, for example, untitled, undated speech by Rabbi Nieto in Jacob Nieto Papers, Western Jewish History Center, Berkeley, California. Rabbi Neito explains that women had the duty by nature to shape the moral perceptions of their children, but that since the child's personality was malleable, the mother must be flexible in shaping its character.

45. Alice Gerstle Levison, "Interview" (1967), 17,41, Bancroft Library.

46. Lucile Hening Koshland, "Interview" (November 1 & 15, 1968), 10-11, Bancroft Library.

47. Seattle Ladies Hebrew Benevolent Society, Minute Book, March, 1896, Manuscript Collection, University of Washington Library.

48. Toll, *Making Ethnic Middle Class*, 49-50.

49. Toll, *Making Ethnic Middle Class*, 52.

50. Toll, "A Quiet Revolution: Jewish Women's Clubs and the Widening Female Sphere, 1870-1920," *American Jewish Archives*, XLI, 1 (Spring/Summer, 1989), 9-10.

51. William Toll, "Gender, Ethnicity and Jewish Settlement Work in the Urban West," in Jeffrey Gurock and Marc Lee Raphael, eds., *An Inventory of Promises, Essays on American Jewish History in Honor of Moses Rischin* (Brooklyn,1995), 299-306.

52. Jessica Peixoto to Milicent Shinn, July 12, 1896, Milicent Shinn Papers, Bancroft Library.

53. Toll, "Gender, Ethnicity and Jewish Settlement Work," 296.

Promises, Promises: The Jewish Romance with America

Jenna Weissman Joselit

American Jews who came of age in the first half of the twentieth century were unabashed in their affection for the New World. Time and again – in 1909, with the Broadway debut of Israel Zangwill's romantic melodrama, "The Melting-Pot;" in 1933 with the opening of the mass public spectacle known as "The Romance of A People;" and, in 1954-55, during a year-long celebration of the 300th anniversary of Jewish settlement in the United States – they made lavish use of the rhetoric of romance to express their gratitude and fidelity to America. These three events (and many others just like them) dramatize just how deeply American Jews had fallen in love with America.

Courting couple

National Museum of
American Jewish History
Gift of Maxine Kam

Cupid Finds A Way

With its pretty parks and broad boulevards, romantic restaurants and glittering nightspots, the modern metropolis abounded in opportunities for "stepping out." Broadway, the "Great White Way," also beckoned to young lovers, especially when the matter at hand and on the boards had to do with the "tug of love." [1] No wonder, then, that courting couples like Anna Brenner and Frank Zimring eagerly awaited the New York debut of "The Melting-Pot," Israel Zangwill's paean to America and the power of love. Fresh from a successful run in Washington, D.C., where it earned the applause and plaudits of the highest-ranking theatre goer in the land, President Theodore Roosevelt, the four-act, "racial play" took up residence in a "pretty little gray and rose playhouse," the Comedy Theatre, on West 41st Street. [2] "Call it sentimental, hysterical, melodramatic, clap-trap, what you will, the fact remains that ["The Melting-Pot"] grips you, thrills you and that is a sufficiently rare achievement in modern drama to insure success," trilled one of the play's many enthusiasts. [3]

Jewish audiences, comprised mainly of the sons and daughters of immigrants, seemed particularly to agree. At home on the set's "curious blend of shabbiness, Americanism, Judaism and music," with its "mouldering" Hebrew books, grand piano, and prints of Lincoln, Columbus and the Wailing Wall, Jewish theatre goers saw themselves, not actors, up on stage.[4] They recognized their fathers in the persona of Mendel Quixano, the well-meaning but ineffectual *balebus*, and their mothers in the character of Frau Quixano, the fierce, unyielding matriarch of the family, forever wedded to the Old World and its ways. Their hearts aflutter, they identified with David Quixano, a sensitive, "sunny, handsome youth of the finest Russo-Jewish type," who transcends his tragic past to become an accomplished American composer.[5] ("So your music finds inspiration in America," David is asked. "Yes," he replies, "in the seething of the Crucible.")[6]

Rooting for the beautiful and highborn Vera, the non-Jewish "Spirit of the Settlement house" who falls madly in love with David, Jewish audiences embraced the America that made such passion possible.[7] "Cling to me, despite them all, cling to me until all the ghosts are exorcised, cling to me till our love triumphs over death. Kiss me. Kiss me now," David implores his beloved Vera. He urges her to let bygones be bygones and, as one critic would have it, challenges Cupid to have his way despite seemingly insurmountable odds.[8] But Vera resists. "I dare not! It will make you remember." To which David replies, "No, it will make me forget. Kiss me." Eventually, as the audience holds its collective breath, awaiting the inevitable denouement, the couple kisses, setting in motion a remarkable *coup de theatre*: the sun sets in a blaze of color, the torch of the Statue of Liberty "twinkles over the darkening water," while, in the distance, a chorus is heard singing "My Country, 'tis of Thee," as the curtain falls gracefully to the floor.[9]

With such a happy ending, it was no surprise that both the romantically inclined and the civic minded applauded "The Melting-Pot." Through its artful fusion of romantic love and patriotism, this play, declared one enraptured viewer, is "likely to make every man and woman who hears it a better American and every immigrant, whatever his fate here, feel a new sense of privilege and the possibility of citizenship."[10] Said another, "The Melting-Pot" is "calculated to do for the Jewish race what *Uncle Tom's Cabin* did for the colored man."[11]

New York's community of sharp-tongued theatre critics, however, stood apart from all the ballyhoo.[12] "The Melting-Pot," they claimed, was not a play but a "lecture in four acts," or, worse still, a "sermon," intended more for the "ethnologist than the playgoer." Overly preachy and didactic, this "second-rate drama" was riddled with "platitudinous Americanisms," way too much sighing, and excessive displays of "false sentimentality." The only thing lacking, charged the critics, was a plot. Zangwill is "under the momentary hallucination that he is a trifle superior to dramatic law," sneered the influential *Theatre Magazine*, wondering what had possessed the veteran playwright to sacrifice plot for atmosphere and color, while the *New York Times,* in what was perhaps the harshest criticism of all, damned the play as "claptrap patriotism," a "mere sop to the groundlings."[13]

Without the imprimatur of the critics, the future of "The Melting-Pot" seemed ill fated. Thanks, though, to the support of the "groundlings," or the "subway public," as they were known in more contemporary circles, "The Melting-Pot" ran for a respectable, though by no means exceptional, one hundred and thirty six performances before travelling on to Chicago.

Although it failed to make theatre history, the play enjoyed the kind of afterlife rarely granted even the most successful of theatrical vehicles. In the months and years that followed, the concept of "the melting pot" took hold in America, becoming one of the most enduring cultural slogans of the 20th century. Together with David, Vera, Uncle Mendel, and Grandma Quixano, countless Americans would affirm their belief that "America is God's Crucible, the great Melting-Pot where all the races of Europe are melting and re-forming! A fig for

Rooting for the beautiful and highborn Vera, the non-Jewish "Spirit of the Settlement house" who falls madly in love with David, Jewish audiences embraced the America that made such passion possible.

your feuds and vendettas! Germans and Frenchmen, Irishmen and Englishmen, Jews and Russians – into the Crucible with you all! God is making the American." [14]

Other Americans, most notably American Jewry's leading opinion-makers, were not so quick to fan the fires of America's crucible by endorsing intermarriage. Distinguishing between assimilation, which was all to the good, and mixed marriages, which were not, American Jewry's representatives staunchly upheld the Jewish community's long-standing marital taboo. Marriage outside of the faith, they insisted, was not a "synonym of broadmindedness" but a "willful rupture with a revered religion" and a "thrilling past." [15] "It's no feeling of narrow separatism, racial pride or unreasoning exclusiveness that makes the Jew oppose mixed marriage," Rabbi David de Sola Pool would explain some years later in an extended analysis of the phenomenon. Rather, it all has to do with "the instinct for self-preservation." [16]

"The Melting-Pot," ca. 1909. Robert D. Rubic, photographer

The White Studio Collection, The Billy Rose Theatre Collection, New York Public Library for the Performing Arts

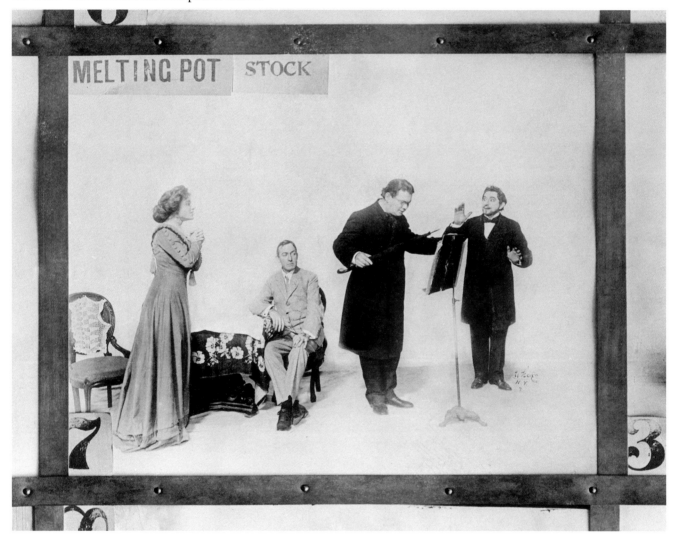

Zangwill, however, understood things differently – or so claimed American Jewry's leaders. The playwright (himself a partner in a mixed marriage) confused assimilation with intermarriage, charged the *American Hebrew,* one of New York's most prominent Anglo-Jewish newspapers. He had failed to see that the "melting process does not apply to the religious beliefs of the immigrants. The Roman Catholic does not cease to be a Roman Catholic because he became American." [17] Echoing the *American Hebrew*'s stance, the *Hebrew Standard* also took vigorous exception to Zangwill's celebration of love. "That a Jew marries a Christian may be only his private affair; that America of necessity demands that the Jew shall intermarry is not founded upon truth." [18]

But then "truth" had very little to do with it. On stage and off, "The

Melting-Pot" made a very vivid, poignant, and at times irresistible case for the primacy of love, casting it as a symbol of America's promise. Intermarriage, when seen from this perspective, was no longer the ultimate act of betrayal but the very heart of patriotism. It is no wonder, then, that American Jewish audiences responded warmly to "The Melting-Pot." In applauding the union of David and Vera, they were applauding their beloved America.

A Romantic People

Whereas "The Melting-Pot" played out the drama of belonging on a small, intimate scale, "The Romance of A People," a musical pageant that told "the story of the Jewish race from away back when," was nothing short of spectacular.[19] With a cast of thousands singing, dancing and gesturing their way through 4000 years of Jewish history, "The Romance of A People," declared its creator, cultural impresario Meyer Weisgal, "is not intended to be doctrinaire… it attempts to prove nothing. It is intended as a huge show."[20]

Despite Weisgal's disclaimer, "Romance" was not simply an entertaining divertissement. "Colossal" in scope, the pageant purposefully romanticized Jewish history, seeking to impress Americans from all walks of life with its majesty and grandeur. Nine elaborately staged scenes or "outstanding historical epochs" spanning the dawn of Jewish history in the Garden of Eden to its denouement, in modern-day Palestine and America, repeatedly and vividly made the point that the history of the Jews was a history of passion.[21] As it moved from the old world to the new, from the medieval era into modernity, culminating in scenes of America, "Romance" also seemed to suggest that Jewish history experienced its apotheosis in Chicago.

Through the "wedding of three art forms – drama, dance and oratorio –" spectators vicariously walked with Abraham, suffered through slavery in Egypt, and rejoiced in the glory that was Jerusalem's. They experienced centuries of exile as well as a period of "peace and culture" in Spain, and endured years of homelessness in Europe, only to find the possibility of redemption in Palestine and fulfillment and freedom in America. Fire-breathing idols and scantily clad chorines added to the spectacle.[22]

In its earliest avatar, "The Romance of A People" was intended as the finale to "Jewish Day," a celebration of the Jewish "contribution" to Chicago's Century of Progress Exposition and, amid growing anti-Semitism in Germany, a "magnificent gesture to fling in the face of a Hitler."[23] Following its Chicago debut on July 3, 1933, "Romance" traveled first to New York, then to Philadelphia and Detroit. It returned to Broadway, considerably reduced in scale, in 1934.

"Seldom have the theatrical arts been called upon to mold so vast a production," one eyewitness recalled. "Never before have so many theatrical and musical notables collaborated on one presentation."[24] Under the artistic direction of Isaac Van Grove, a director of the Chicago Civic Opera; Jacob Ben-Ami, the actor; choreographer Louis Chalif and architect Peter Clark, the "world's largest stage" was filled with dancing girls and "bacchanalians," priests in "bejeweled breastplates" and joyful Hasidim who portrayed the "aspiration, conflict, pity [and] love" that was characteristic of the Jewish historical experience.[25] The pageant format, explained the profoundly theatrical Weisgal ("P.T. Barnum had nothing" on him, it was said),[26] had traditionally been considered a "sort of auxiliary enterprise… an orphan, a plaything, a game, an amusing trifle for the ladies or for the young folk." But "Romance," he insisted, was about to change all that, paving the way for the pageant to become a "permanent technique in Jewish education and propaganda."[27]

From top to bottom, everything about "The Romance of A People" was oversized and extravagant. This drama, prospective ticket-buyers were breathlessly informed, is "breath-taking in its scope, beautiful in its artistry, conceived by genius and executed by masters."[28] Take its stage, for example. "Those who saw... its beauty, its immensity, were awe-stricken and stood there in bewilderment... The stage is a piece of work which will remain in Jewish history for generations."[29] Rising "tier by tier," the stage actually consisted of three connecting units, each with its own elaborate series of stairs and terraces: an altar in the shape of a six-pointed Jewish star; the "center field" some 150 feet in diameter; and a tableau of Jerusalem and its Temple. The last, measuring 120 feet high, towered over the stadium's bleachers and, in some spots, even "obliterated" the tracks of the Chicago "el." [30] Meanwhile, underneath the stage, a "vast army" of carpenters, electricians and technicians used the most sophisticated telephone, lighting and audio equipment, including a highly touted "electro-acoustical apparatus" thought to be a precursor of stereo sound, to keep things humming.[31] That modern technology was brought to bear on the past, on a time when "electric lights, telephones and switchmen never existed," furthered a collective sense of marvel and delight.[32]

Program for "The Romance of a People," 1933

National Museum of American Jewish History

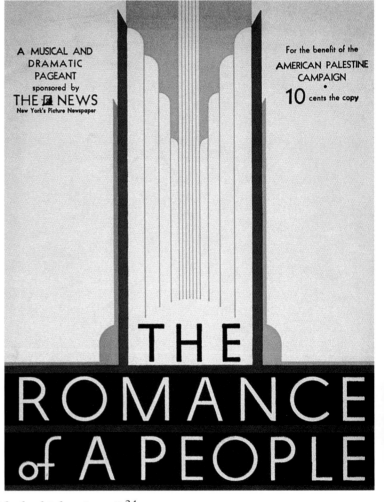

A MUSICAL AND DRAMATIC PAGEANT
sponsored by
THE ◾ NEWS
New York's Picture Newspaper

For the benefit of the
AMERICAN PALESTINE CAMPAIGN
•
10 cents the copy

THE ROMANCE of A PEOPLE

Above ground, the cast – an unusual mix of amateurs and theatre professionals – made history come alive. "Hatred of Hitler, not Pharaoh," inspired the performance of one dancer, Frances Chalif, a "lithe, blond, Slavic-featured" woman who fancied scarlet lipstick and English cigarettes, and who played Miriam, Moses' "sturdy sister." Interviewed by ace reporter Joseph Mitchell on the eve of her Chicago debut, Chalif said that "as she danced she would not think of the Egyptians whose horses were drowned in the Red Sea but of brown-shirted Germans rolling down the *Kufurstendamm* in motor trucks."[33]

Thousands of lay performers – school children, stenographers, debutantes, and the unemployed – apparently shared Chalif's sentiments and volunteered their time and energy to the production. "There is an element of romance in the very staging of this gigantic spectacle," noted the *American Hebrew*. "The modern stenographer is to relive the past of thousands of years ago. The modern office clerk is to parade and strut the stage as a Roman centurion or walk in solemn assembly with the high priests." [34] Stiff and ungainly as scarecrows, the amateur cast of centurions and priests was eventually transformed under Van Grove's gentle, patient prodding into a disciplined and graceful "cavalcade of Jewry." [35] "When they began, these youngsters had no more idea of the dynamics of a dramatic pageant than they had of Asiatic history," observed Judge Harry Fisher, the general chairman of "Jewish Day," referring to the hundreds of Hebrew school student volunteers. But after weeks of rehearsal, "they made the impression of being steeped in the tradition of the orient. They had rhythm, grace and discipline. They had caught the spirit of the production." [36]

"Jewish Day" generated a great deal of publicity as well as public spirit. "Many a heart will beat faster in anticipation," declared one onlooker, while another reported that New York Jewry was simply "agog with excitement." [37]

Closer to home, local newspapers, especially the *Chicago Jewish Chronicle*, a "weekly paper for the modern Jewish home," whipped up and sustained enthusiasm for "Jewish Day" through a steady diet of editorials, features, and fancifully drawn advertisements about the event, reportedly the "biggest and most impressive exhibition of Jewish genius ever undertaken."[38] "There must be no let-up in the sale of tickets and in the endless chain of propaganda which every man and woman can start for themselves," insisted the *Chronicle*, while pundits predicted that "Jewish Day is a tremendous event that will live long in the memory of every Jew."[39] The Erie Railroad, in turn, sought to ensure such memories by providing specially-priced trains like the "Weizmann Special" to whisk passengers to the Windy City from as far away as Memphis, Pittsburgh and New York. "Take your seat at 'The Romance of A People,'" urged the pageant's producers. "It will make you proud that you are a Jew and that you have lived to see this great spectacle."[40]

Pride, coupled with a kind of cultural defiance not usually seen among

Scene from "Romance of a People," 1933

Weizmann Institute of Science, Rehovot, Israel

American Jews, brought thousands to the fair grounds. Breaking all attendance records, over 125,000 visitors set the "turnstiles whirling," as they gathered to listen to speeches from such luminaries as Chaim Weizmann, to attend conferences on "interfaith amity," and to watch their children compete in athletic contests.[41] Come nightfall, eager spectators "jammed" Soldier Field, waiting for "The Romance of A People" to sweep them off their feet.[42] "The portrayal of the 'Romance' is itself woven into the Romance," said one observer, clearly moved by the occasion. "Here we are more than 100,000 Jews, the largest Jewish assemblage since Temple days."[43] "What a night!" exclaimed another.[44]

Despite the augustness of the occasion, not everyone enjoyed herself. Indeed, if post-performance comments from "earnest onlookers" are a reliable guide, the actual experience of "Romance" fell woefully short of most everyone's expectations.[45] For one thing, the stage was so far away from the audience – often at a distance equivalent to two city blocks – that the performers looked like "pinheads." For another, many in the bleachers found their view of the proceedings blocked by lighting poles and broadcasting horns: "We couldn't see a thing."

Some who could see simply didn't like what they saw. What happened to America and the Statue of Liberty, disappointed pageant-goers wanted to know, questioning the organizers' last-minute decision to shorten the production's running time. "Why was the part America has played in the lives, happiness, and opportunities of almost five million Jews cut?" Others, meanwhile, wondered why the pageant concluded with "a group of flag-waving, Sunday school kids running onto the stage, helter-skelter" rather than with a dignified salute to the beloved statue, that icon of America. Was this ending intended to convey the message that the future resided in (flag-waving) children? Still others complained that "The Romance" lacked warmth: a "triumph of remote broadcasting," it had more in common with an "exaggerated Reform synagogue service" than it did with the panoramic realities of Jewish history.

While a disappointment in some Chicago circles, "Romance" aroused considerable interest in New York. With the financial backing of Colonel Patterson and his newspaper, the *Daily News,* and the civic backing of Mayor John P. O'Brien, it was decided that a "rewritten, revamped and rearranged" version of the Biblical pageant would be brought to the Bronx.[46] "It was altogether unlikely" that "The Romance of A People" would not be seen in New York, the mayor explained, "for this city contains more people of Jewish blood than ever were brought together in any city in their long history."[47] Not only did "Romance" enjoy a repeat performance but so, too, did "Jewish Day." Declaring September 14, 1933 "Jewish Day" in the Big Apple, O'Brien hailed the special day as "an expression of appreciation to a group of our fellow citizens who have contributed greatly to the cultural advance and the material progress of our city."[48] As the carillon of Riverside Church pealed in celebration and a squadron of airplanes flew over City Hall in salute, enthusiasm mounted. "History will become drama next Thursday evening," predicted the *New York Times,* and labeled the event, which was scheduled to open at the famed Polo Grounds, home to the New York Yankees, "ball park pageantry."[49]

But weather of epic, even Biblical proportions wreaked havoc with the pageant's debut, forcing its cancellation. Heavy rains flooded the Polo Grounds, transforming the ballpark into a lake on the surface of which floated ruined bits of scenery depicting millennial moments in Jewish history.[50] Weisgal and his supporters anxiously casted about for a new venue. They found a home for "Romance" at the "largest armory in the world" – the Bronx-based 258th Field Artillery – and feverishly began transforming its drill space into a "modern theatre of vast proportions."[51]

Despite the unanticipated change in venue, New Yorkers came in droves to see the much-heralded pageant. "Nearly a million people came, by subway, by bus, by car and on foot," Weisgal recalled.[52] Some of those who made their way to the Bronx were simple folk, hungering for a glimpse into "the glamorous, tragic panorama of Israel's past." Others included prominent men of the cloth like Reverend Harry Emerson Fosdick of Riverside Church and Reverend Milo Gates, dean of the Cathedral of St. John the Divine. Also in attendance were equally prominent men of the celluloid screen such as Harry Warner of Warner Brothers and Samuel Katz of Paramount Pictures, whose presence led to rumors that Hollywood was considering a cinematic version of the pageant.[53] "It has been an inspiring and deeply impressive spectacle,"

American Jews of the interwar years, having fallen in love with America a generation earlier, were now free to fall in love with their own culture.

Reverend Gates related, allowing how, given his druthers, he would have named the pageant, "The Romance of A *Romantic* People." "It has been very interesting not only to the men and women of the Jewish lineage but to every student and lover of the Old Testament."[54]

An "unprecedented success" in the Big Apple, the pageant then traveled to Convention Hall in Philadelphia, where it was again plagued by the weather: a blizzard this time around.[55] But ticket-holders in the City of Brotherly Love – like those in the Big Apple – persevered. Little could dampen the spirits of the estimated 70,000 who braved mounds of snow to see the show. Later still, a "smaller and more compact" version of "Romance" returned to Broadway and the fabled Roxy Theatre just in time for Rosh Hashannah 5694.[56] *Variety* helpfully pointed out that "'Romance' fits the present occasion of the Jewish holidays as aptly as nuns and church singing at the Roxy during Christmas and Easter."[57] The pageant was performed four times every weekday and five times a day on Saturday and Sunday.

Ultimately, with all the talk of romance in the air and on the stage, "The Romance of A People" marked a dramatic turning point in American Jewish history. American Jews of the interwar years, having fallen in love with America a generation earlier, were now free to fall in love with their own culture. Infatuated, if only momentarily, with the romance of Jewish history and its relevance to America, they renewed their bonds to the past and to each other. As one participant put it in the summer of 1933: "Thank God for Jewish Day! At 'A Century of Progress,' on the eve of America's great day of Independence, the Jew portrays his eternal Romance – his Romance with God, with life, with ideals."[58]

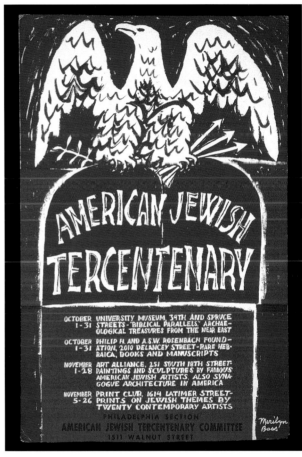

Tercentenary Poster

National Museum of American Jewish History Gift of Maxwell Whiteman

Happy Anniversary

In the wake of World War Two, American Jews turned once again to history, reaffirming their love of the past. This time, though, it wasn't the Biblical era, the Golden Age of Spain or even the recent destruction of East European Jewry that stirred their emotions, but the 300th anniversary, or Tercentenary, of Jewish settlement in the United States. "A kind of spiritual birthday," the event occasioned a year-long period of intensive "rejoicing and stock-taking," during which American Jews, confident and optimistic about their future, happily laid claim to an American, rather than an ancient, past.[59] The Tercentenary, explained one of its organizers, "offers a fruitful opportunity for both an appraisal of... Jewish self-fulfillment in the setting of American freedom and an accounting of what American Jews have done with their freedom."[60]

From September 1954 through June 1955, over four hundred Jewish communities throughout the nation celebrated their "spiritual birthday" with concerts, exhibitions, fashion shows, lectures, pageants, and prayer services. Blurring the lines between high and low culture and between elite and populist forms of commemoration, the Tercentenary gave birth to the "greatest mass observance ever conducted by American Jews in their 300 year history."[61] Jewish Los Angelenos, for instance, marked the occasion with a "dramatic cavalcade and a Bible lecture" while St. Louis Jewry dedicated a "Tercentenary flagpole." In other cities and towns throughout the country, American Jews built new synagogues, sponsored "important historical displays," listened to concerts of Jewish music and attended a special Tercentenary Sabbath service designed to coincide with the weekend of Thanksgiving, that most American of invented traditions. They also watched television. Each of the major networks featured programs – panel discussions, interview shows and dramatizations – which "brought the story of Jewish participation in American life to the eyes and ears of millions."[62] The season's highlights included "Night of Vigil," a "vivid" dramatization of the first Passover held on American soil, and "The Cow that Coughed," the story of philanthropist Nathan Straus' efforts to ensure an affordable supply of pasteurized milk for the poor of New York.[63]

        From the quotidian to the sublime, every manifestation of the Tercentenary spirit sought to underscore the compatibility of Judaism with America. "In its American aspects, it is fitting for this Tercentenary to assume a patriotic tone – not in a superficial flag-waving spirit, but rather in the sense that all Americans hold a deep and often unspoken love for their country and its people," declared a Tercentenary publication entitled "Scope and Theme." "It is equally fitting," continued the report, referring to the Jewish "aspects" of the celebration, "that we recognize, not in self-glorification but in self-respect, the good things that we as a group have brought to America... We have brought a love of the arts and a respect for those who create with words and sounds and colors... With our all-too intimate knowledge of persecution, we have brought a deep passion for human freedom and personal dignity."[64]

        To get that "complementary" message across required considerable human and financial resources. The American Jewish Committee, American Jewry's leading defense organization, supplied both in equal measure by spearheading the formation of the American Jewish Tercentenary Committee.[65] With its own staff of public relations specialists, art directors, writers and historians, the American Jewish Tercentenary Committee reminded American Jews of the power of the past while assuring them of the integral relationship between Jewish and American history. As one official document put it, "In the life of the American Jew it is and has always been *natural and proper* for him to be an American and a Jew." [66]

        In the hopes of balancing the two, the Tercentenary Committee published its own newsletter, *300*, replete with details on the celebration. It also issued a series of pamphlets such as "Everyman's Guide to the American Jewish Tercentenary," that suggested ways to best commemorate the anniversary. The committee's recommendations included taking family trips to sites of Jewish interest, and staging a pageant, a cantata or a "costume ball," and awarding prizes for the "most imaginative costumes based on the early life of the Jewish settlers in America." Creating some kind of audio-visual program to which children will "respond warmly" was another suggestion.[67] To further the celebratory spirit, the Tercentenary Committee also designed a special

Romance was a popular theme on Jewish New Year's greeting cards distributed in America.

National Museum of American Jewish History, Mr. and Mrs. Howard Yusem Purchase Fund

commemorative poster featuring an American eagle entwined with a menorah. "Simple [and] effective," this poster "is fully in keeping with the dignity of the observance. It is especially designed for display in synagogues and temples, community centers and Y's, halls, churches, stores and bank windows."[68]

But then, the Tercentenary was intended to be more than just fun and games. Commissioning leading American historians such as Harvard University's Oscar Handlin to write about the American Jewish experience and encouraging communities at the grassroots to do much the same thing, the Tercentenary Committee sought to develop and sustain American Jewry's historical awareness. After all, fidelity to the past was an American attribute. To be an American, explained David Bernstein, executive director of the Tercentenary Committee and one of its ablest chroniclers, is to engage in an "unceasing search for identification with the American past," and to believe that "it is a greater honor to have had an ancestor on the Mayflower than on Noah's Ark." American Jews, he hastened to add, "supplement the authentic American impulse to publicize the antiquity of *their* roots in this country with the desire to remind themselves and their Christian neighbors that these roots made each of them as clearly American as the most stately daughter of the American Revolution."[69]

Through it all, the Tercentenary underscored the primacy of the folk, in ways rhetorical and performative. This celebration, American Jews were told time and again, is your celebration; it "belongs primarily to five million people who regard themselves as patriotic, loyal American Jews, whatever their definition or their philosophy."[70] Apparently, quite a number of American Jews – perhaps all five million of them – took such statements to heart by weighing in, now and then, with comments and criticisms of their own. True to form, some insisted the celebration was "too Jewish;" others, that it wasn't "Jewish enough." Still others believed the Tercentenary minimized secular forms of *yidishkayt* and scanted the contribution of Yiddish to American culture, while another segment of the population believed the event smacked too much of secularism. Then there were those who felt that the celebrations were "too Zionistic" while others thought they weren't Zionist enough. Cause for dismay in some quarters, American Jewry's heterogeneity was embraced in others as a characteristic reflection of the community's "healthy fermentation of ideas."[71]

Some institutions also preferred to chart their own course. The Council of Jewish Women, for example, elected to "make its own special contribution" by commissioning a study of the Jewish family in America.[72] In contemporary America, wrote the study's author, anthropologist (!) Natalie Joffe, "an essential quality that may be called Jewish continues to be apparent, carrying on certain values and traditions that have come down through the years. It is this basic design, often elusive, that this study attempts to trace." Eager to discuss as well as to trace, various chapters or "sections" of the council devoted symposia to and held lectures on the Jewish family as well as on kindred themes such as intermarriage and "self-acceptance."[73] Council women in Schenectady and Washington, D.C. embarked on even more imaginative forms of programming. They sponsored historical pageants such as "Our Shining Heritage," and produced an historically sensitive fashion show, "The March of Council," which featured samples of clothing worn by council women over the six decades since the organization's inception in the 1890s.[74]

When it came to display, celebrants took to exhibitions, "a most attractive medium," with especially great relish.[75] In high school hallways and public library lobbies as well as in the venerable galleries of New York's Metropolitan Museum of Art and the Jewish Museum, American Jewish history was made manifest in varied ways. Jewish women in Norfolk, Virginia, for example, organized a flower show featuring "floral displays" arranged in ancestral "heirloom containers" while in

This celebration, American Jews were told time and again, is your celebration; it "belongs primarily to five million people who regard themselves as patriotic, loyal American Jews, whatever their definition or their philosophy."

New York, the Board of Jewish Education put together an exhibition entitled "Sweet Land of Liberty," with murals, ceramics, mobiles and dolls that offered a "colorful interpretation by the children of American Jewish history."[76] The Met, in turn, played host to "Art of the Hebrew Tradition," a display of approximately one hundred and fifty ceremonial objects, including a number of "delightfully contrived spice containers."[77]

Meanwhile, art of a different kind was on view at the Riverside Museum in New York, the Albright Art Gallery in Buffalo and Washington's Corcoran Gallery of Art, thanks to a travelling show called "The Contemporary Fine Arts Exhibit of the American Jewish Tercentenary." Featuring works by Jewish luminaries of the art world such as Raphael Soyer, Max Weber, Adolph Gottlieb, and Philip Reisman as well as paintings and sculpture by less well-known "contemporary American artists of Jewish background," the show was intended to reflect "in stone and wood and metal, on canvas and paper... the opportunities for cultural development in our country."[78] This is "art worth celebrating," wrote the cultural critic William Schack, intimating that the exhibition had lived up to its mandate. On display is a "group show of unusually sustained quality. Not only were most of the older and invited guests represented by good examples, but there were some thirty to forty meritorious pieces by artists whose names are known only to assiduous gallery-goers."[79]

By far the most popular and heavily trafficked of all Tercentenary related exhibitions, and perhaps even "the most important event of the year," was "Under Freedom," a history show mounted by the Jewish Museum.[80] Filling three floors of the former Warburg mansion (itself a "typical example of Jewish Americana," as one reporter put it), "Under Freedom" traced the history of American Jewry from the arrival of Columbus through the "drama-packed exodus" of Eastern European Jewry centuries later.[81] To tell this complex story, explained curator Stephen Kayser, "the exhibit seeks in itself to be a work of art, appealing to the broadest possible number of visitors. It stresses the visual and understandable, rather than the esoteric or the rare. It stresses the positive aspects of the social history of American Jews – the shared experience, the common denominator, the universal emotion."[82]

Upon entering the museum, visitors were greeted by an "impressionist representation of Columbus" fashioned out of wire, cardboard and sheet metal; a sword purportedly carried by one of Columbus' men hung nearby.[83] War souvenirs were prominent – Uriah Levy's weapon was another featured attraction as were the "mementoes of Jewish military chaplains." The exhibition also contained a replica of the Liberty Bell, a reconstruction of the sanctuary of Charleston's historic K.K. Beth Elohim, original documents from the archives of the Council of Jewish Women and a sampling of photographs, medals and trophies belonging to Jewish athletes "whose names are still in the headlines."[84] Moreover, at a time when many American Jews had come to believe that the "land of nostalgia" was no longer

"A Small Wedding, But a Happy One." In this extraordinary play on patriotism and marital fidelity, the bride, representing a new American citizen, marries Uncle Sam.

Der Groyser Kundes
(New York, 1911)
Courtesy of Peter H. Schweitzer

Eastern Europe but the lower East Side, "Under Freedom" assuaged their longing for authenticity through a series of "representative" vignettes, among them the "spotlessly clean simple room of a tenement building," and a "typical Lower East Side street scene," complete with a pushcart and Yiddish theatre posters.[85]

Whatever their motivations or intentions, visitors thrilled to the "vivid and detailed visualization" of three centuries of American Jewish history and left the museum feeling "uplifted and inspired."[86] Lively and colorful, "Under Freedom" placed American Jewish history within reach: as one delighted visitor exclaimed, it is "now within the grasp of everyone to take in the complete panorama of American Jewish history since Columbus in less than two hours."[87]

Commanding attention, the American Jewish Tercentenary received a great deal of play in circles outside of the American Jewish community. "Protestants Note 300th Anniversary," American Jews observed with justifiable pride. "Possibly for the first time in American history, Protestant churches in New York City... played "Kol Nidre" on their chimes on the eve of Yom Kippur... [as] an expression of good-will."[88] In yet another manifestation of good will, David Rockefeller was widely quoted as saying that the Tercentenary "held deep significance... for lovers of democracy everywhere."[89] Always welcome, such sentiments vindicated American Jewry's belief that the Tercentenary was not only an event "broad enough to appeal to 160,000,000 Americans," but, more gloriously still, a "happy anniversary" that sealed the union of America and its Jews.[90]

Over the years, American Jews have relied on an unusually diverse and inventive array of cultural strategies through which to express feelings of belonging, attachment, and affection for their country. Turning to objects and song, dance and stagecraft, they have endowed each one with a distinctive rhetorical sensibility – the language of love. This quintessentially American language, with its references to personal happiness, fulfillment, and promise, enabled American Jews to give voice to their growing collective sense of happiness, fulfillment, and promise. Perhaps more importantly, the language of love enabled them to affirm their identity as Americans and as American Jews, and at the same time to affirm the harmony – the essential rightness – of such a union. When seen in this golden light, who's to say American Jewish history isn't romantic?

Notes

1. "The Tug of Love," *Current Literature,* Vol. 43 October 1907, pp. 461-3.

2. Unidentified clipping, January 24, 1910, The Billy Rose Theatre Collection of The New York Public Library of the Performing Arts. This collection contains dozens of unattributed clippings and genizah-like fragments of articles in a folder marked "Clippings -- The Melting-Pot." (Hereafter, this collection is referred to as BRTC.) See also Arthur James review of "The Melting-Pot," unidentified newspaper, ca. 1909, BRTC.

3. "The Tragedy of Kishineff: Israel Zangwill's 'Melting-Pot,'" *American Hebrew,* September 10, 1909, p. 467.

4. The description of the set is Zangwill's own. See, for example, Israel Zangwill, *The Melting-Pot: A Drama in Four Acts* (New York: The Macmillan Co., 1909), p. 2.

5. "Melting-Pot," op. cit., p. 29.

6. "Melting-Pot," op. cit., p. 37.

7. Ibid.

8. The passages cited in this paragraph are drawn from "Melting-Pot," op. cit., p. 197, and from BRTC.

9. "Melting-Pot," op. cit., p. 199.

10. Fragment of clipping, January 24, 1910, BRTC.

11. Liebler & Co., "Endorsements from the President, the Statesmen, [and] the Clergy of Mr. Walker Whiteside in "The Melting-Pot," (Chicago, n. d.), p. 22, BRTC.

12. What follows is drawn from a selection of clippings found in BRTC.

13. *Theatre Magazine* Vol. X, No. 104, October 1909, p. 106; Adolph Klauber, "A Spread Eagle Play by Israel Zangwill," *New York Times,* September 12, 1909, p. 10.

14. "The Melting-Pot," op. cit., p. 32.

15. "Cupid in Shackles," *American Hebrew,* June 16, 1905, p. 69.

16. Reverend Dr. David de Sola Pool, "Intermarriage," *Hebrew Standard*, February 7, 1919, p. 6.

17. "The Melting-Pot," *American Hebrew*, September 10, 1909, p. 476.

18. "Zangwill's 'The Melting-Pot,'" *Hebrew Standard*, September 10, 1909, p. 8.

19. *Variety,* September 11, 1934, n. p. The Billy Rose Theatre Collection of the New York Public Library for the Performing Arts also contains a series of folders pertaining to the performance history of "The Romance of A People." (Hereafter cited as BRTC-2).

20. Weisgal quoted in "Ball Park Pageantry," *New York Times,* September 10, 1933, Section 10.

21. "Thousands Prepare To Take Part in 'The Romance of A People' Pageant," *American Hebrew,* September 8, 1933, cover page; see also, *New York Times,* August 31, 1933, p. 17.

22. Jacob Ben-Ami, "Welding Untrained Amateurs into a 'Cavalcade of Jewry,'" *New York Herald Tribune,* September 10, 1933, BRTC-2; "Ball Park Pageantry," op. cit.

23. "The Romance of A People Inspiring," *American Hebrew,* September 29, 1933, p. 319.

24. "Thousands Prepare to Take Part," op. cit., p. 245.

25. "125,000 See Drama of Israel at Fair," *New York Times,* July 4, 1933, p 16; *New York Evening Post,* October 14, 1933, n. p., BRTC-2.

26. "Sidelights," *Chicago Jewish Chronicle*, July 7, 1933, p. 16.

27. Meyer Weisgal, "The World's Greatest Assemblage of Jews," *Chicago Jewish Chronicle,* June 30, 1933 p. 3.

28. "Jottings by H.L.M.," *Chicago Jewish Chronicle,* June 2, 1933, p. 16.

29. "A Century of Progress," *Chicago Jewish Chronicle,* June 2, 1933, p. 16.

30. "125,000 See Drama of Israel at Fair," op. cit.; "Pageant To Use Biggest Setting Ever Designed," *New York Herald Tribune,* August 29, 1933, n. p., BRTC-2.

31. "The Pageant of The Jewish People," *New York Times,* September 25, 1933, p. 3.

32. Judge Harry Fisher, "Chicago Builds A Pageant," *Chicago Jewish Chronicle,* June 9, 1933, p. 3.

33. Joseph Mitchell, "Hatred of Hitler, Not Pharaoh, Will Inspire Dancer," *New York World-Telegram,* September 5, 1933, n. p., BRTC-2.

34. "Thousands Prepare to Take Part," op. cit., p. 245.

35. Jacob Ben-Ami, "Welding Untrained Amateurs," op. cit.

36. Judge Harry Fisher, "Chicago Builds A Pageant," op. cit.

37. "Kaleidoscope by Abram," *Chicago Jewish Chronicle,* June 9, 1933, p. 8; Benjamin Weintraub, "Jewish Day Items," *Chicago Jewish Chronicle,* June 30, 1933, p. 7.

38. "Kaleidoscope by Abram," *Chicago Jewish Chronicle,* June 9, 1933, p. 8..

39. Ibid.; *American Hebrew*, June 30, 1933, p. 122.

40. "Kaleidoscope by Abram," *Chicago Jewish Chronicle,* June 16, 1933, p. 8.

41. "Chicago Fair Crowd Sets Mark With Over 200,000," *New York Times,* July 4, 1933, p. 16.

42. Meyer Weisgal, *Meyer Weisgal...So Far – An Autobiography* (New York: Random House, 1971), p. 112.

43. "The Romance of A People Souvenir Programme," July 3, 1933, BRTC-Programmes.

44. "Kaleidoscope by Abram," *Chicago Jewish Chronicle,* July 7, 1933, p. 8.

45. The following critical remarks were culled from several articles published in the *Chicago Jewish Chronicle*. They include Earnest Onlooker, "From One of Those Present," July 7, 1933, p. 2.; "Kaleidoscope by Abram," July 14, 1933, p. 8; "Jottings by H.L.M.," July 14, 1933, p. 16; "Sidelights," July 7, 1933, p. 16.

46. "Jottings by H.L.M.," July 14, 1933, p. 1.

47. "Tonight's Pageant," *New York Times,* September 14, 1933, p. 22.

48. *New York Times,* September 5, 1933, p. 11.

49. "Ball Park Pageantry," *New York Times,* September 10, 1933, op. cit.

50. "Rains Cause Transfer of Jewish Pageant From Open," *New York Herald Tribune,* September 16, 1933, BRTC-2.

51. " Jewish Pageant Will Open Tonight," *New York Times,* September 24, 1933, Section 2, p. 1.

52. Weisgal, *Weisgal... So Far,* op. cit., p. 115.

53. "The Romance of A People Inspiring," *American Hebrew,* September 29, 1933, p. 319.

54. Reverend Gates quoted in *New York Times,* October 9, 1933, n. p., BRTC-2 (author's emphasis).

55. "Run Extended through October 19th," *American Hebrew,* October 13, 1933, p. 365.

56. "The Romance of A People Revived at Theatre," *New York Herald Tribune*, September 8, 1934, n. p., BRTC-2.

57. *Variety*, September 11, 1934, n. p., BRTC-2.

58. Solomon Goldman quoted in "The Romance of A People Souvenir Programme," op. cit., n. p.

59. "Local Activities from Coast to Coast," *300*, No. 21, November 1954, p. 23.

60. "American Jewish Tercentenary Programs for Youth Groups: Themes and Program Emphases," 1954, Archives of the Jewish Theological Seminary of America, RG 11, Communications Department, Box 62, Folder 25, "Tercentenary of American Jews," 1954.

61. David Bernstein, "The American Jewish Tercentenary," *American Jewish Year Book,* Vol. 57, 1956, p.118. What follows is drawn from the Bernstein article as well as from information published in *300*, the Tercentenary newsletter.

62. "Jottings by H.L.M.," July 14, 1933, p. 1.

63. "Tonight's Pageant," *New York Times,* September 14, 1933, p. 22.

64. Excerpts from "Scope and Theme" can be found in Bernstein, "American Jewish Tercentenary," op. cit., p. 103.

65. Ibid.

66. Cited in Nina Warnke, "The American Jewish Tercentenary," unpublished paper presented at the 60th Annual YIVO Conference, October 1988 (author's emphasis). I'd like to thank Ms. Warnke for graciously sharing her paper with me.

67. "American Jewish Tercentenary Programs for Youth," op. cit., pp. 4-5.

68. *300*, No. 18, August 1954, p. 1.

69. Bernstein, "American Jewish Tercentenary," op. cit., pp. 101-2.

70. Excerpt from "Scope and Theme," in Bernstein, "American Jewish Tercentenary," op. cit., p. 103.

71. See, for example, Bernstein, "American Jewish Tercentenary," op. cit., p. 103.

72. "We Celebrate Tercentenary," *Council Woman*, Vol. 16, No. 2, April 1954, p. 8.

73. Natalie Joffe, *The American Jewish Family: A Study* (New York: Council of Jewish Women, 1954), Preface. See also *Council Woman*, Vol. 17, No. 1, January 1955, p. 10.

74. *Council Woman*, Vol. 17, No. 1, January 1955, p. 11.

75. "American Jewish Tercentenary Programs for Youth Groups," op. cit., p. 4.

76. *Council Woman*, Vol. 17, No. 4, May 1955, p. 12; *New York Times*, April 12, 1954, Clipping in Jewish Theological Seminary of America Scrapbook, No. 29, "Tercentenary Scrapbook."

77. "Hebrew Art Shown by Met," *New York World-Telegram*, January 22, 1955, n. p., Jewish Theological Seminary Scrapbook, No. 29.

78. American Jewish Tercentenary Committee, "The Contemporary Fine Arts Exhibit of the American Jewish Tercentenary," (New York 1955), n. p.

79. William Schack, "Art Worth Celebrating," *Commentary*, October 1955, p. 337. Though Schack was certain of the artistic merits of the work on display, its imputed identity -- as Jewish art -- was something else again. "What, now, do all these artists mean as a Jewish group?" he wondered. "For myself the blunt answer must be that they have no meaning in this sense, whether they are judged by the idiom in which they work, their subject matter, or the Jewish feeling they may -- or may not, as I think -- display."

80. David Horowitz, "The Tercentenary Exhibit," *Chicago Sentinel,* December 23, 1954, n. p., Jewish Theological Seminary Scrapbook, No. 29.

81. William Goldman, "300 Years of Jewish Life in the United States Shown at Museum," *New York Mirror,* November 21, 1954, Jewish Theological Seminary Scrapbook, No. 29.

82. Stephen Kayser, "Under Freedom," Jewish Museum Exhibition Catalogue, 1954, Jewish Theological Seminary Archives, RG 25, The Jewish Museum, Box 7.

83. What follows is drawn from "Under Freedom," as well as from various clippings found in Jewish Theological Seminary Scrapbook, No. 29. These clippings include pieces in the *New York Herald Tribune,* November 24, 1954; *Jewish News of Detroit,* November 26, 1954; *American Hebrew*, April 29, 1955; and *JWB Circle,* December 1954.

84. *New York Herald Tribune,* November 24, 1954.

85. Shack, "Art Worth Celebrating," op. cit, "300 Years," op. cit.

86. Horowitz, "Tercentenary Exhibit," op. cit.

87. Ibid.

88. "Protestants Note 300th Anniversary," *300*, No. 21, November 1954, p. 6.

89. "David Rockefeller Notes Milestone's Implications," *300,* No. 18, August 1954, p. 9.

90. Excerpt from "Scope and Theme," in Bernstein, "American Jewish Tercentenary," op. cit., p. 103.

Jewish Identity, Assimilation' and Multiculturalism

David A. Hollinger

In America, one can be Jewish in several, different, equally valid ways, and no one, regardless of his or her ancestry, can be told by this or that authority, that he or she is, or is not, a Jew.

When Secretary of State Madeleine Albright was confronted in 1997 with press accounts that her parents had been Jewish, she found herself in the middle of an animated conversation about Jewish identity in the United States. Albright had grown up without any knowledge of her Jewish ancestry; the truth had been concealed by her parents, who had fled Hitler's Europe and become Catholics. But Albright, who was approaching sixty, was living in a society where Jews were not persecuted. She was free to be as Jewish as she cared to be. She might even embrace Judaism, and renounce the Episcopalian affiliation she had maintained since the time of her marriage. But she did not change her religion, and she showed no interest in any ethnic or cultural variety of Jewishness. To the disappointment of some, Albright appeared to be unchanged by the news of her Jewish ancestry. Indeed, she was so detached from this part of her past, that she awkwardly denied that she had learned of it privately some time before it became public. Hundreds of news articles and editorials addressed what *The New Republic* called "Madeleine Albright's Jewish problem." [1]

Madeleine Albright

Corbis-Bettman

Is Madeleine Albright "really" Jewish? If so, in what sense? Can one be of "Jewish background," as Albright came to describe herself,[2] but not be "Jewish"? Who decides, and on what basis? What is at stake, and for whom? "There are," as Jews often say at Passover, "many questions."

But there are also answers. Or, at least in the minds of some people, not all of whom would agree with one another, there are answers. For instance, many Rabbis, from ancient times to the present, could handle these questions easily. So, too, could Adolph Hitler, and officials in Vichy France. Arab diplomats are quite clear; the new American Secretary of State is Jewish, they say, and they are ready to take this into account when considering her position on diplomatic issues. No doubt the Supreme Court of Israel could come to equally confident conclusions. Yet for many people in Albright's own place and time – the United States of the late-twentieth century – these questions resist ready answers, and can be difficult even as they apply to Americans who, unlike Albright, think of themselves as Jewish.

What renders these questions challenging is a widespread feeling that in America, one can be Jewish in several, different, equally valid ways, and that no one, regardless of his or her ancestry, can be told by this or that authority, that he or she is, or is not, a Jew. To describe this attitude as "widespread" is not to say everyone endorses it. On the contrary, the debate about Jewish identity includes voices that condemn this extreme voluntarism, those that cite the authority of Jewish law, and some that invoke specific rules such as the principle that any child born of a Jewish mother is a Jew. Some of the most earnest voices advising on what Jewish identity should mean are motivated by a concern for the survival of the Jewish people under conditions that invite the dissolution of traditional bonds. Yet it is this robust voluntarism – expressed in the very notion that certain varieties of Jewishness appropriate to modern America can be "invented"– that defines the terms of the discussion.

What features of American society and culture in the late twentieth century turned the discussion of Jewish identity in this direction? Three were of overwhelming importance.

First, the political dynamics of World War II incalculably strengthened an old Enlightenment ideology according to which individuals are to be as free as possible from the negative effects of ascribed social distinctions. The victorious struggle against racist regimes in Europe and the Pacific discredited discrimination against Jews and other stigmatized groups within the United States.

Second, the resulting openness of American society to Jews who maintained a strong Jewish identity, as well as to those who did not, facilitated a measure and scale of socioeconomic integration virtually unprecedented in the Diaspora. Unlike France, Germany, and other nations that had, in one epoch or another, offered the full benefits of national life to Jews at the price of conversion to Christianity or at the price of other diminutions of Jewishness, the United States after World War II was relatively undemanding. In many respects it actually encouraged Judaism as part of a pluralistic religious front against the "Godless communism" of the Cold War. Hence, as Jews made their way into the mainstream of American economic, political, and cultural life, the distinction between Jews and other groups was not sharply marked, and assimilation proceeded at a ferocious pace. By the 1980s, conservative estimates revealed that well over one-third of marrying Jews acquired non-Jewish spouses. Some credible surveys put this figure at over one-half.

Grand and boldly modern in design, postwar synagogues like Shaarey Zedek in Southfield, Michigan, were symbols of Jewish affluence and security.

Balthazar Korab, photographer

Third, the ethnoracially plural character of American society, consisting of a variety of European communities of descent as well as those derived from Africa, Asia, South America and North America itself, yielded a discourse about assimilation and group identity that was very different from that of Britain, Italy, France, Germany, the Netherlands and most other nations. In those countries, Jews as a group were defined primarily in relation to a single "host" group that had a long-standing proprietorship of the nation and its geographical territory. Yet in the United States, Jewish identity came to be considered in relation to identities such as African-American, Italian-American, Irish-American, and Japanese-American, the contingent character of which became apparent by the 1980s when Jews were absorbed, for many purposes, into an amorphous "European-American" identity. In this dynamic demographic context, a mystique of Jewish uniqueness apart from religious Judaism was much more difficult to maintain, and the entity into which Jews were assimilating kept changing.

Additional historical circumstances helped shape the question of Jewish identity in the United States. These include the existence of the state of Israel, for example, and the memory of the Shoah. But the influence of these and other conditions is best understood within the framework of the three foundational features of the situation of Jews in recent American history introduced above: Enlightenment ideology, socioeconomic integration, and ethnoracial plurality. These features of post-1945 America did much to create the atmosphere conveyed lucidly by a leading historian of modern American Jewry:

> the largest, wealthiest, and most powerful community in the history of the Diaspora, confronted the challenge of freedom and opportunity. There now seemed hardly any honor or position in American life for which [Jews] could not aspire... Gentiles enjoyed the movies of Woody Allen, they made best sellers out of *Marjorie Morningstar, Exodus, Portnoy's Complaint,* and other books with Jewish themes, and they helped Harry Golden become a Jewish Will Rogers. A black comedienne by the name of Caryn Johnson even thought it would benefit her career if she changed her name to Whoopi Goldberg. This openness of American society also meant that there were few external influences forcing Jews to affirm a sense of Jewishness. *Jews would continue being Jews because they wanted to, not because they were being forced to.*[3]

The voluntarism with which this passage climaxes is worth underscoring: in the United States in the second half of the twentieth century, Jews were not forced to be Jews, but could maintain their Jewish affiliation "because they wanted to." And the society as a whole showed less and less interest in keeping track of who wanted to, and who did not. Many Rabbis, Jewish intellectuals, and members of Jewish organizations pondered the fate of the Jews as a distinctive people in the wake of emancipation.[4] However, very little attention was paid to this question by an American society which, until the middle of the 1940s, had tolerated extensive restrictions on the employment, education, housing, and recreation of Jews. Sociologists sometimes kept track of the numbers of religious or ethnic Jews – or those simply possessed of a Jewish name – in various walks of life, as did some Jewish agencies charting the welcome decline of anti-Semitism. But in most professions, colleges, neighborhoods, and resorts, people proved increasingly oblivious to who was Jewish and who was not. A line that had meant so much to so many in so many contexts suddenly blurred in the era immediately following World War II. In no sector was this change more dramatically manifest than in academia.

Jews had been systematically excluded from many faculties before World War II, but by the end of the 1960s about 17% of the combined faculties of the nation's leading universities identified themselves on a questionnaire as Jewish. The liberal arts college of Yale University hired its first Jewish professor in 1946; in the early 1970s its faculty was about one-fifth Jewish. Since Jews constituted only about 3% of the American population, this amounted to an "overrepresentation" by more than 500%. Nationally, self-identifying Jews constituted more than one-third of the faculties in some disciplines at the elite universities. A 1969 study by the Carnegie Commission found, for example, that within the seventeen most prestigious universities, Jews made up 36% of the professors of law and 34% of the professors of sociology. Even in the humanities, where the exclusion of Jews had been the most severe on the grounds that these culturally strategic fields could not be entrusted to persons lacking a Christian background, Jews accounted for 22% of the historians and 20% of the philosophers. Never in American academic history had any group made such a rapid and statistically spectacular transition from being a largely excluded minority to being overrepresented by, in some fields, more than 1000%.[5]

Beyond academia, Jews were prominent in demographically disproportionate numbers in many social and economic sectors. "During the last three decades," reported Seymour Martin Lipset and Earl Raab in 1995, Jews have made up

> Forty percent of American Nobel Prize winners in science and economics... 40 percent of partners in the leading law firms of New York and Washington, 26 percent of the reporters, editors, and executives of the major print and

Many Rabbis, Jewish intellectuals, and members of Jewish organizations pondered the fate of the Jews as a distinctive people in the wake of emancipation.

broadcast media, 59 percent of the directors, writers and producers of the fifty top-grossing motion pictures from 1965 to 1982, and 58 percent of directors, writers, and producers in two or more primetime television series.[6]

Information of this kind is sometimes offered – with much justice – simply as a celebration of the accomplishments of an immigrant ethnic group in the New World. It is offered here, however, to point out how open American society proved to be to individuals of Jewish ancestry once the old, Anglo-Protestant establishment began to apply to Jews an individualist and egalitarian ideology – the same ideology about which this establishment had been so hypocritical in the past. Hasidic Jews publicly distinguished themselves from the rest of society, but Jews of other kinds, whether involved in Jewish communal life or altogether separated from it, found that their Jewishness was not noticed in ways that prevented them from accomplishing the same things their comparably-equipped, gentile fellow-citizens could.

This reality, firmly established by the middle of the 1960s, set the stage for an unprecedented increase in intermarriage. This ultimate form of assimilation became easier once the line between Jews and gentiles had faded in less intimate settings. In 1940, when the line was still quite distinct in much of the nation's institutional space, only about 3% of Jews who married were marrying gentiles. By the end of the 1960s, the figure had risen under the changing, post-war circumstances sketched above, to 11%. And by 1990, the National Jewish Population Survey found that 57% of Jews who had married during the previous five years had acquired a non-Jewish spouse.[7] This figure was contested, which yielded another round of debate over who should and should not be considered Jewish. Was a groom or bride who had only one ethnically Jewish parent, and who had never been initiated into Judaism be counted as an outmarrying Jew if he or she married someone who was not Jewish? On questions such as these turned the matter of whether Jewish outmarriage had reached the astonishing percentage claimed by the National Jewish Population Survey. But if the exact figure was in dispute, the basic reality was not: Jews were outmarrying in rapidly increasing numbers.

Many other ethnoracial groups in the United States were also outmarrying at a high rate. Hence, the issue of Jewish identity and survival became bound-up with the issue of group identity and survival of many, diverse segments of the population. The presence of these other ethnoracial groups is a crucial aspect of the Jewish experience in modern America. This is a factor not always grasped by those who have considered the issues of Jewish assimilation in relation to the very different societies of Germany, France, Italy, or Great Britain.

Public discourse of the 1970s and 1980s was enlivened by arguments about the character and significance of the ethnicity of the old, European immigrant communities. This was partly but not exclusively in response to the public attention given to black Americans in the wake of the civil rights legislation of the 1960s. Some sociologists suggested that the "fever of ethnicity" displayed by many Irish, Italian, and other "white ethnics" amounted to merely a "symbolic ethnicity" by which highly assimilated Americans maintained a sentimental tie to a communal past that was not, in fact,

As early as the late 1940s, Jewish communal leaders worried about the consequences of assimilation and economic success.

LOOK *magazine, 1954.*
National Museum of
American Jewish History

THE VANISHING AMERICAN JEW

Contradiction: While more Jews than ever before are participating in religious affairs, marriages outside the faith are increasing at an "alarming" rate.

Leaders fear threat to Jewish survival in today's "crisis of freedom"

■ New studies reveal loss of Jewish identity, soaring rate of intermarriage.
■ Judaism may be losing 70 percent of children born to mixed couples.
■ Because of low birthrate, Jews are "scarcely reproducing themselves."
■ Jews may fade from 2.9 to 1.6 percent of U.S. population by the year 2000.

42 LOOK 5-5-H

operating in their daily lives.[8]

Varieties of group survivalists resisted this interpretation. They continued to quote the legendary 1963 assertion of Nathan Glazer and Daniel Patrick Moynihan that the significant thing about the melting pot was that "it did not happen." [9] But every ten years, census data confirmed not only the existence of but also the growth, and hence the formidable power, of the melting pot. Thus, questions about the perpetuation of ethnic cultures were rendered unavoidable. The 1990 census data revealed that 81% of married Polish-Americans between the ages of 25 and 34, and 73% of married Italian-Americans of the same age cohort, had married outside their ethnic group. Even some non-European communities of descent were assimilating quickly. About half of the 24-35 year-old Asian-Americans who had been born in the United States were marrying non-Asians, about 60% of Native Americans were acquiring non-Native American spouses, and approximately one-third of Latinos were marrying outside the Latino demographic

IT'S EXCITING TO BE ESTONIAN

Bumper stickers like this one affirmed the ethnic categories of the 1970s.

Balch Institute for Ethnic Studies

bloc. While intermarriage rates were substantially lower for black Americans – about 3% of black women were marrying white husbands, and about 8% of black men were marrying white wives – these figures for 1990 were themselves striking; until only twenty-three years earlier, black-white marriages had been illegal in most of the states with the largest percentage of black residents.[10]

The debates over African-American identity had an especially strong influence on the atmosphere in which American Jewish identity was discussed in the 1970s, 1980s, and 1990s. This may seem paradoxical, given that black-white marriage rates were so much lower than the comparable rates for Jews, and that blacks and Jews were distributed, for the most part, at the opposite ends of the class structure. But traditional Jewish strategies for maintaining communal solidarity under adverse conditions recommended themselves to black leaders frustrated with the slow pace of integration. The concept of the "diaspora," associated primarily with Jews, was widely adopted to refer to the situation of black people outside the continent of Africa, and especially to the situation of black people in the United States. The seasonal ritual of Kwanzaa, invented in 1972 by African-American political activist Ron Karenga (and by the 1980s, routinely given extensive attention in public schools), is a Seder-like celebration that resembles Passover much more than the ethnically undifferentiated Christian holiday of Christmas.[11] Within the background of both of these innovations was the long-standing, symbolic identification of African-American slaves and their descendants with the Biblical Jews as slaves in Egypt. Analogies in the historical experiences of blacks and Jews had often been drawn, moreover, by Jews who had been conspicuous among the white Americans who had devoted political energy to the diminution of prejudicial treatment of blacks from the Progressive Era through the 1960s. Not in Germany, France, Italy, England, or even in multi-ethnic Russia, had a community of Jews worked out its relationship to a national society while symbolically paired with another "minority group" that was several times its demographic size yet many times weaker in economic power, and that was uniquely central to the national history – the focal point, indeed, of a civil war.

The most sweeping change to the setting in which the identity of the Jewish group was addressed in the United States was brought about by the historic situation of this special American sibling group–African-American. This is the replacement of the religiously-coded "triple melting pot" popularized by Will Herberg's best-selling sociological classic of 1955, *Protestant-Catholic-Jew,*[12] with the color-coded "ethnoracial pentagon" of the 1980s and 1990s. As long as religion loomed large in the discussion of group identity in the United States, Jews were certain to be allotted important space as the carriers of one of the world's great religions. But a religiously-centered analysis that did not distinguish sharply between the destinies of black Protestants and white Protestants left much of the American social experience egregiously out of account. Trying to take account of the differential experience of black and white Americans proved to be the major agenda of social observers in the United States during the twenty years following the publication of Herberg's book. Hence the religious categories used by Herberg became less and less salient. Commentators on the American scene became convinced that color was the social distinction that most affected the destiny of individuals. The point about Jews, in this context, is that they were white. But Americans were not to be divided into two categories, black and white, and Jews were not to debate the identity question in relation to this simple distinction. Instead, three events intervened to produce a five-part structure. According to this structure, every individual is said to be an African-American, an Asian-American, a European-American, a Latino, or a Native American.[13]

First, the Immigration Reform Act of 1965 opened the way for massive immigration from Asia and Latin America. Millions of Chinese, Korean, Vietnamese, Guatemalan, El Salvadorian and Mexican immigrants – as well as those from other countries – suddenly diversified an ethnoracial map that had been altered little since the restrictive legislation of the mid-1920s. New groups appeared, and groups already present found their numbers greatly augmented. Although the majority of "Hispanics"– especially those from Mexico – identified themselves as "white," the Spanish language and brown skin color distinguished most of these "Latinos," as they came to be called, from the European-derived segments of the white population. Immigrants from East Asia, in the meantime, fell more obviously into a non-white racial category, for which the term "oriental" had been in use since the earlier term "Mongoloid" had fallen out of fashion along with nineteenth-century race theory. The rapid upward social mobility and assimilation of several Asian ethnic groups led to the notion that these Asians were being "whited" in much the same way that Irish, Polish, Jewish, and other non-Anglo European groups had been gradually incorporated into "white America." But most immigrants from East Asia were undoubtedly "yellow," in the same crude sense that most immigrants from Latin America were "brown." The demographic picture was complicated somewhat by the immigrants from South Asia. Called "black" in Great Britain, their color was actually closer to "Latino brown" than to "Oriental yellow," but they did not share the Spanish language, and their official racial classification in the discredited but still influential theories of the nineteenth century, was "Caucasian."

Second, several of the historically disadvantaged minority groups built political movements modeled on those developed by blacks during the 1960s. Prominent among these were Latinos, some of whom lobbied to have the census bureau designate them as a "race" rather than as an ethnic group within the white race. American Indians, too, pursued an "identity politics" designed to call attention both to their cultural contributions and to the extent of their mistreatment in the past and present by empowered whites. Some organizations

As long as religion loomed large in the discussion of group identity in the United States, Jews were certain to be allotted important space as the carriers of one of the world's great religions.

speaking on behalf of Asian-Americans as a whole, or on behalf of specific Asian ethnic groups, also surfaced. Hence the inventory of political movements to advance the interests of historically disadvantaged groups was expanded. Ethnoracial politics in the United States went beyond black and white demographic blocs (or "races," as some would still insist), to include brown, red, and yellow.

Third, the role of these color-categories in American life widened during the 1980s and 1990s in the wake of constitutional impediments to affirmative action and other color-specific entitlements sought by some of the movements mentioned above. In the 1978 Bakke decision of the United States Supreme Court, it was determined that preference for one "race" over another in school admissions was legitimate if designed to achieve cultural diversity. Justice Lewis Powell declared that the nation needed leaders exposed to "the ideas and mores of students as diverse as this Nation of many peoples."[14] The result was that affirmative action programs could be defended if individual members of each group being awarded preference – black, brown, red, or yellow, as the case may be – had

You don't have to be Jewish

to love Levy's
real Jewish Rye

distinctive "ideas and mores." This, in turn, gave enormous impetus to the movement for cultural diversity in education that soon came to be called "multiculturalism." Multiculturalism had other roots too, and it extended well beyond higher education. But multiculturalism developed hand-in-hand with affirmative action, yielding the impression that culture followed color. Remarkably, multiculturalism has been oblivious to religiously defined cultures, mostly because it serves as a cultural surrogate for color-specific remedies for past and present discrimination. If the point was culture, not color, then it made excellent sense to stop talking about "whites" and "blacks," and to instead talk about "European-Americans" and "African-Americans." This is exactly what the public was encouraged to do, with the result that the most gross and invidious of notions of what makes human beings different from one another have been advanced under the cover of sensitivity to geography and history.

Levy's advertising campaign implied that Jews had lost their ethnic distinctiveness, as many things Jewish were absorbed into mainstream American culture.

National Museum of American Jewish History

Hence American Jews were surrounded by a discourse about group identity in America that presented a number of features with special implications for Jews. The discussion systematically de-emphasized religion, yet for Jews the religious component of identity was of enormous significance. This discourse privileged color, yet color did not distinguish the overwhelming majority of Jews from white people in general. This discourse resisted the notion that any one group had a loftier historical destiny than any other, yet Jews, even while accepting the pluralistic, egalitarian ethos of the contemporary United States, were, after all, heirs to a tradition in which the myth of the "chosen people" was exceptionally vivid. This discourse downplayed the linguistic and historical particularity of communities found within one or another of the color-coded blocs, yet for Jews, linguistic and historical particularity were basic to group identity. This discourse nested issues of identity firmly in a matrix of unequally distributed power, and often aspired to allocate social benefits on the basis of demographically proportional representation, yet Jews were the richest and most empowered of any of the society's standard "minority groups."

There were compelling reasons for the triumph in the 1980s and 1990s of such a discourse of identity. The point here is not to fault the structure of this discourse. It is to clarify the public atmosphere in which one particular white community of descent necessarily discussed identity. This community had associated with it a distinctive religion, it had a sense of choseness, and it had experienced persecution of apocalyptic dimensions – but not under the direct ordinance of the United States. The Jewish group was now firmly established amid the most prosperous and empowered of their fellow-citizens. Thus it stood to lose prodigiously if it were suddenly subjected to a politics of "representation" according to which educational and employment opportunities were distributed proportionately on the basis of group membership.

The situation was complicated further by the existence of the state of Israel. Many American Jews felt some measure of loyalty to this foreign state that served as a "home" to an American "diasporic" community. But Israel was not quite the political and moral equivalent of Mexico, nor of the several African and Asian nations in relation to which other American "diasporas" were defined. Israel, moreover, was engaged in an enduring struggle with Arab and Muslim nations that were the suppliers of increasing numbers of American immigrants, and hence the "home" in relation to which yet more American "disaporic" communities were defined.

And this brings us back to Madeleine Albright, the American Secretary of State whose Jewish identity was no mystery to diplomats in Damascus and Cairo. Albright's situation can remind us of a distinction often ignored in discussions of "identity": the distinction between ascription and affiliation. Anyone can ascribe Jewish identity to Albright by regarding her as a passive object, invoking in relation to that object one or more of the criteria by which she is a Jew. But only she, as a willing subject, can affiliate as a Jew, and to whatever extent and by whatever means she chooses.[15] Affiliation is no less important to Jewish identity in America today than is ascription, and as long as American Jews are free to "invent" their Jewishness, this will continue to be true

Notes:

For helpful suggestions based on a draft of this essay, I want to thank my colleague, Robert Post.

1. Martin Peretz, "Human Condition," *New Republic,* March 10, 1997, 29.

2. This is Albright's construction in a statement she read at the ancient Jewish cemetery in her ancestral Prague, as reported in the *New York Times,* July 14, 1997, 1.

3. Edward S. Shapiro, *A Time for Healing: American Jewry Since World War II* (Baltimore, 1992), 256. Emphasis added.

4. On the ambiguities of the concept of "emancipation," see the Introduction (esp. 4-5) of a splendid collection of studies of the process of Jewish emancipation, Pierre Birnbaum and Ira Katznelson, eds., *Paths of Emancipation: Jews, States, and Citizenship* (Princeton, 1995).

5. The results of the Carnegie study are found in Stephen Steinberg, *The Academic Melting Pot: Catholics and Jews in American Higher Education* (New York, 1974), esp. 101-103, 122-123. For Yale, see Dan A. Oren, *Joining the Club: A History of Jews at Yale* (New Haven, 1985), esp. 261-268, 326. For an overview of the transformation of Jewish intellectuals from a marginalized group to a dramatically overrepresented segment of the academic establishment, see David A. Hollinger, *Science, Jews, and Secular Culture: Studies in Mid-Twentieth Century American Intellectual History* (Princeton, 1996), esp. 7-11.

6. Seymour Martin Lipset and Earl Raab, *Jews and the New American Scene* (Cambridge, Mass., 1995), 26-27.

7. For these studies and an analysis of them, see Richard Alba, "Assimilation's Quiet Tide," *Public Interest* (Spring 1995), esp. 15.

8. Herbert Gans, "Symbolic Ethnicity in America," *Ethnic and Racial Studies* II (1979), 1-20.

9. Nathan Glazer and Daniel Patrick Moynihan, *Beyond the Melting Pot* (New York, 1963).

10. See Matthijs Kalmijn, "Trends in Black/White Intermarriage," *Social Forces* LXXII (September 1993), 119-146. State laws prohibiting black-white marriages were ruled unconstitutional in *Loving v. Virginia,* in 1967.

11. For a thoughtful review of the history and significance of Kwanzaa by a prominent black writer ambivalent toward it, see Gerald Early, "Dreaming of a Black Christmas," *Harpers* (January 1997), 55-61.

12. Will Herberg, *Protestant-Catholic-Jew: An Essay in American Religious Sociology* (New York, 1955).

13. For a fuller account of the ethnoracial pentagon and its historical context, see David A. Hollinger, *Postethnic America: Beyond Multiculturalism* (New York, 1995), esp. 23-50.

14. Justice Powell's words can be found in his opinion, within *Regents of University of California v. Bakke,* 483 U.S. 265 (1978), 311-313.

15. For a provocative recent contribution to the discussion of ascribed and chosen identities, see Katya Gibel Azoulay, *Black, Jewish, and Interracial: It's Not the Color of Your Skin, but the Race of Your Kin, and Other Myths of Identity* (Durham, N.C., 1997).

A checklist of the Exhibition

BEGINNINGS

"The English Empire in America"
London, ca. 1685
map
reproduction
Rare Book Division, The New York Public Library
Astor, Lenox and Tilden Foundations

The Port of New Amsterdam
Laurens Block, artist
1650
watercolor
reproduction
New York Historical Society

Portrait of Moses Raphael Levy
Gerardus Duyckinck, artist
New York, ca. 1720-1728
oil on canvas
Museum of the City of New York
Bequest of Alphonse H. Kursheedt

View of the port of Savannah
by P. Fourdrinier, 1734
engraving after Peter Gordon
reproduction
Library of Congress

The Port of Philadelphia
Peter Cooper, artist
ca. 1720
oil on canvas
reproduction
Library Company of Philadelphia

Newport, Rhode Island
lithograph (1884, after a 1740 overmantle painting)
John P. Newell, artist
reproduction
Newport Historical Society

Portrait of Aaron Lopez
Newport, RI, ca. 1752
pastel on paper
reproduction
American Jewish Historical Society
New York City, NY and Waltham, MA

Hanukkah lamp
Carribbean (probably Curacao)
early 18th century
embossed and chased silver
National Museum of American Jewish History
Gift of Dr. and Mrs. Frederick Greenwald
Conservation made possible by the Stephen A.
Ritt, Jr. Memorial Fund

NEW WORLD

Plan of Spruce Street Cemetery
John Lukens, Surveyor General
Philadelphia, October 31, 1765
ink sketch
Congregation Mikveh Israel, Philadelphia

Account book of David Franks
Philadelphia, 1755-1761
reproduction
American Jewish Historical Society
New York City, NY and Waltham, MA

Drawing of "Jew's Synagogue"
William Strickland, architect
Philadelphia, 1824
ink and waterolor
reproduction
Congregation Mikveh Israel, Philadelphia

Circumcision record book of Barnard I. Jacobs
Heidelberg, PA, ca. 1765
ink on vellum
Congregation Mikveh Israel, Philadelphia
Conservation made possible through The Pew
Charitable Trusts Museum Loan Initiative

Torah Finials *(Rimmonim)*
Myer Myers, silversmith
New York, ca. 1772
embossed and chased silver, partial gilt, cast ornaments
Congregation Mikveh Israel, Philadelphia

"Subscription for the Redemption of Strangers"
Philadelphia, 1795
Congregation Mikveh Israel, Philadelphia

Sampler with Hebrew characters
signed SGM
1813
cotton embroidery on linen
National Museum of American Jewish History
Gift of Mr. and Mrs. Lawrence Blumenthal
Conservation made possible by the Stephen A.
Ritt, Jr. Memorial Fund and Mrs. Louis Foster

View of Lancaster, Pennsylvania
ca. 1800
etching
reproduced from Gerald S. Lestz,
The Artists' Album
(Ephrata, PA: Science Press)

**Traveling Torah Scroll and Ark
of Joseph Simon**
Lancaster, PA, ca. 1771
vellum manuscript, silk mantle
Congregation Mikveh Israel, Philadelphia

Ark Lintel from Joseph Simon's home
Lancaster, PA, mid 18th century
reproduction
American Jewish Historical Society
New York City, NY and Waltham, MA

***Shohet's* certificate of Solomon Etting**
Philadelphia, April, 1782
reproduction
Congregation Mikveh Israel, Philadelphia

***Haggadah* of Belle [Bilah] Simon**
London, 1770
A. Alexander, translator
American Jewish Historical Society
New York City, NY and Waltham, MA

Portrait of Michael Gratz
Isaac L. Williams, artist
Philadelphia, 1893
National Museum of American Jewish History
Gift of Congregation Mikveh Israel, Philadelphia

Portrait of Miriam Gratz
Isaac L. Williams, artist
Philadelphia, 1893
National Museum of American Jewish History
Gift of Congregation Mikveh Israel, Philadelphia

Wedding Fan of Belle Simon
New York, 1779
Congregation Mikveh Israel, Philadelphia

Wedding Slippers of Belle Simon
Reuben Bunn, New York, 1779
Congregation Mikveh Israel, Philadelphia

Compass of Michael Gratz
18th century
Congregation Mikveh Israel, Philadelphia
Gift of Kathleen Moore

**Non-Importation Agreement
of Philadelphia Merchants**
October 25, 1765
signed manuscript
Historical Society of Pennsylvania

Note of payment to Barnard and Michael Gratz
signed Joseph Simon
Lancaster, December 19, 1784
American Jewish Historical Society
New York City, NY and Waltham, MA

Letter, Moses Michael Hays to Michael Gratz
Boston, March 16, 1786
American Jewish Historical Society
New York City, NY and Waltham, MA

The port of Newport
1795
Samuel King, artist
L. Allen, engraver
engraving
reproduction
Newport Historical Society

Shipment Instructions for voyage to Curacao
signed Aaron Lopez
Newport, July 8, 1773
reproduction
American Jewish Historical Society
New York City, NY and Waltham, MA

Shipment Instructions for voyage to Barbados
signed Aaron Lopez
Newport, December 14, 1772
reproduction
American Jewish Historical Society
New York City, NY and Waltham, MA

Shipment Instructions for voyage to Quebec
signed Aaron Lopez
Newport, September 12, 1769
American Jewish Historical Society
New York City, NY and Waltham, MA

Business ledger of Aaron Lopez
Newport, 1766-1775
Newport Historical Society

Model of Touro Synagogue
Stuart Gootnick, designer
Niles, Illinois, 1979-84
National Museum of American Jewish History
The Mr. and Mrs. Robert Saligman Purchase Fund

Sermon of Haijm Karigal
printed and sold by S. Southwick
Newport, RI, 1773
National Museum of American Jewish History
Gift of Alfred Bader

Bill of Lading for "Jew Beef"
shipped by Aaron Lopez
Newport, 1771
American Jewish Historical Society
New York City, NY and Waltham, MA

Receipt for payment of *tzedakah*
Congregation Nefutzei Israel
Newport, 1755
American Jewish Historical Society
New York City, NY and Waltham, MA

Oath of Naturalization of Aaron Lopez
Boston, 1762
reproduction
Suffolk Collection, Supreme Judicial Court,
Archives and Records Preservation, Boston

Torah scroll
probably Morocco, early 18th c.
ink on deerskin
Congregation Mickve Israel, Savannah

***Wimpel* (Torah binder)**
Savannah, GA, ca. 1794
Congregation Mickve Israel, Savannah

Minute book of Mickve Israel
Savannah, 1790-1851
Congregation Mickve Israel, Savannah

Sheftall family circumcision set
England, ca. 1854
silver and gold instruments, vellum manuscript
American Jewish Historical Society
New York City, NY and Waltham, MA
Gift of Dr. Walter M. Brickner

Rations receipt issued to Mordechai Sheftall
by Col. J. White
Georgia, 1778
National Museum of American Jewish History
Gift of Peter L. Raphael and Susan Raphael Calman

Kiddush Cup of Philip Minis
silver
18th century
Georgia Historical Society, Savannah

Announcement of tavern opening
Abigail Minis
Georgia Gazette, January 19, 1764
reproduction
Georgia Historical Society, Savannah

Letter, Abigail Minis to Mordecai Sheftall
January 11, 1780
reproduction
Georgia Historical Society, Savannah

**Advertisement for the services of
Haym Salomon, broker**
Pennsylvania Packet and Daily Advertiser
Philadelphia, November 1, 1784
reproduction
National Museum of American Jewish History

Portrait of [Bilhah] Abigail Levy Franks
attributed to Gerardus Duyckinck
New York, ca. 1735
oil on canvas
reproduction
American Jewish Historical Society
New York City, NY and Waltham, MA
Gift of Captain N. Taylor Phillips

Letters of Abigail Levy Franks
reproduced with permission from
the American Jewish Historical Society
New York City, NY and Waltham, MA

Prayer for the Country
Richmond, VA, 1789
signed Jacob, son of R. Joshua Cohen
National Museum of American Jewish History
Gift of ARA Services, Inc., Philadelphia, PA, through
the agency of William S. Fishman
Conservation made possible by the Robert Saligman
Charitable Foundation

**Letter, Hebrew Congregations of Philadelphia,
New York, Charleston and Richmond to
President George Washington**
Philadelphia, 1790
Congregation Mikveh Israel, Philadelphia

**Letter of Reply, George Washington to the
Hebrew Congregations of Philadelphia, New York,
Charleston and Richmond**
Philadelphia, 1790
Congregation Mikveh Israel, Philadelphia

Resolution to vacate the seat of Jacob Henry
North Carolina House of Commons
Raleigh, December 5, 1809
North Carolina Department of Cultural Resources

**Pamphlet, "Proceedings in the Legislature of
Maryland on the 'Jew Bill'"**
printed by Joseph Robinson
Baltimore, 1819
American Jewish Historical Society
New York City, NY and Waltham, MA

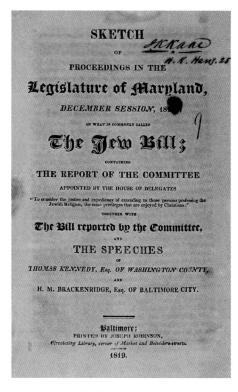

Ledger book, Female Jews Society of Maine
Portland, Maine, 1816-1827
National Museum of American Jewish History

PIONEERS

Battle of the Wilderness
Fredericksburg, VA, 1864
ink sketch
reproduction
Corbis-Bettman

Letter from the front
Myer Levy to his parents
Camp near Deep Bottom, VA
January 24, 1865
National Museum of American Jewish History
Gift of Adelaide Barry

Union Soldier wearing a *yarmulke*
Washington, D.C. ca. 1863
Alexander Gardner, photographer
Courtesy of Robert Marcus

Stagecoach on Toll Road
Boulder Falls, late 19th century
reproduction
Library of Congress

"Plum Street Temple"
Cincinnati, OH, 1866
oil on canvas
Henry Mosler, artist
reproduction
John Reed Forman, photographer
HUC Skirball Cultural Center and Museum

"Denver Station"
ca. 1870
ink sketch
reproduction
Denver Public Library
Western History Collection

Portrait of Louis Anfenger
ca. 1880
reproduction
Beck Archives of Rocky Mountain Jewish History
Center for Judaic Studies and Penrose Library,
University of Denver

Diary of Louis Anfenger
Denver, 1870 - 1872
Beck Archives of Rocky Mountain Jewish History
Center for Judaic Studies and Penrose Library,
University of Denver

Anfenger family portrait
Denver, Colorado, ca.1890
photograph
Courtesy of Marjorie Hornbein

Sampler
by Louise Schlesinger
Albany, NY, 1861
cotton embroidery on linen
Courtesy of Marjorie Hornbein

Card server of Louise Schlesinger Anfenger
engraved silver with the initials "L.A."
Denver, Colorado
Courtesy of Marjorie Hornbein

Framed purse of Louise Schlesinger Anfenger
Denver, Colorado
Courtesy of Marjorie Hornbein

**Advertisement for D.B. Kobey & Co.
closing on "Hebrew Holidays"**
Aspen Daily Times, September 25, 1897
reproduction
Denver Public Library
Western History Collection

**Map, "Mears System of Tollroads,
San Juan County"**
Denver, Colorado
Colorado Historical Society

Portrait of Otto Mears
reproduction
Colorado Historical Society

Otto Mears and Chief Ouray
Colorado, 1868
reproduction
Denver Public Library
Western History Collection

Saddlebags of Otto Mears
leather with fur insets
Colorado Historical Society

Silverton Railroad Pass
issued to Cora Mears
Silverton, CO, 1888
white buckskin
Colorado Historical Society

Rio Grande Southern railroad pass
Silverton Railroad
issued to Mrs. N.P. Hill and family
silver filigree, signed Otto Mears
Colorado Historical Society

**Advertisement for Denver
and Santa Fe Stage Line**
Directory of Trinidad, Colorado for 1888
W. H. Whitney, publisher
reproduction
Denver Public Library
Western History Collection

Commercial Street
Trinidad, CO, ca. 1880
reproduction
Denver Public Library
Western History Collection

Directory of Trinidad, Colorado for 1888
W. H. Whitney, publisher
Trinidad, CO, 1888
Denver Public Library
Western History Collection

Joseph Jaffa Family Picnic
Trinidad, CO, July, 1890
reproduction
American Jewish Archives

Interior of Jaffa Mercantile Company
Trinidad, CO, ca. 1870
reproduction
American Jewish Archives

Interior of Temple Aaron
Trinidad, CO
reproduction
Skirball Cultural Center
Cincinnati Campus

Portrait of Rabbi Freudenthal
Trinidad, CO
reproduction
American Jewish Archives

Letter, S. Levy to Rabbi Louis Freudenthal
National Museum of American Jewish History

***Wimpel* for Abraham Lawrence**
Rabbi Freudenthal, maker
Trinidad, CO, August 15, 1890
painted on linen
Hebrew Union College Skirball Cultural
Center and Museum
Gift of Mrs. Gilbert Sanders

Young peddler with his pack
Ohio, 1860
reproduction
American Jewish Archives

Portrait of Levi Spiegelberg
ca. 1860
reverse photographic image, oil painting on glass
Palace of the Governors Collection
Museum of New Mexico

Portrait of the Spiegelberg Brothers
Santa Fe, New Mexico, ca. 1865-1870
Napoleon Sarony, photographer
reproduction
Museum of New Mexico
Negative no. 11025

Portrait of Betty Spegielberg
ca. 1860
reverse photographic image, oil painting on glass
reproduction
Palace of the Governors Collection
Museum of New Mexico

Passover plate of the Langerman Family
Bavaria, ca. 1800
American Jewish Historical Society
New York City, NY and Waltham, MA

Cane of Abraham Speigelberg
Palace of the Governors Collection
Museum of New Mexico

"Spiegelberg Hermanos" currency
Santa Fe, NM, 1863
reproduction
American Jewish Historical Society
New York City, NY and Waltham, MA

Portrait of Emanuel Rosenwald
O.S. Dowe, photographer
reproduction
Museum of New Mexico
Negative no. 103189

Women's Riding Gloves
leather, stamped "Emanuel Rosenwald, Las Vegas, NM, 1874"
Palace of the Governors Collection
Museum of New Mexico

Inkwell of Noah Ilfeld
ca. 1890
cut-glass with hinged silver lid
Palace of the Governors Collection
Museum of New Mexico

Patent Desk of Charles Ilfeld
Wooton Desk Manufacturing Co.
Indiana, ca. 1880
walnut (Eastlake pattern)
Palace of the Governors Collection
Museum of New Mexico

Charles Ilfeld family
Las Vegas, NM, ca. 1870
reproduction
Center for Southwest Research, Zimmerman Library, University of New Mexico

Ilfeld Building on the Plaza
Las Vegas, NM, ca. 1885
reproduction
Museum of New Mexico
Negative no. 14719

Advertisement for Ilfeld Brothers
Catalog of Fashions
Butterick Publishing Co.
Autumn 1897
Fray Angelico Chavez History Library
Palace of the Governors
Museum of New Mexico

Dedication program, Temple Emanuel
Denver, CO, January 27-29, 1899
Beck Archives of Rocky Mountain Jewish History
Center for Judaic Studies and Penrose Library, University of Denver

Postcard of Temple Emanuel
Denver, ca. 1905
National Museum of American Jewish History

Juliet Friedman with her sisters
early twentieth century
photograph
Courtesy of Sharon Seeman

The Kosher Fair Cookbook
Ladies of Congregation Emanuel, publishers
Denver, CO 1888
reproduction
Beck Archives of Rocky Mountain Jewish History
Center for Judaic Studies and Penrose Library, University of Denver

Minute Book
Denver Lodge of B'nai Brith
Denver, CO, 1879-1886
Beck Archives of Rocky Mountain Jewish History
Center for Judaic Studies and Penrose Library, University of Denver

Mason's Apron of Moritz Bernstein
Wallensberg, CO, ca. 1899
Beck Archives of Rocky Mountain Jewish History
Center for Judaic Studies and Penrose Library, University of Denver

"Kosher Picnic"
National Council of Jewish Women
Denver, CO, ca.1895
reproduction
Beck Archives of Rocky Mountain Jewish History
Center for Judaic Studies and Penrose Library, University of Denver

Memoir of Mrs. Frances Jacobs
Charity Organization Society, publisher
Denver, CO, 1892
Denver Public Library
Western History Collection

IMMIGRANT NEIGHBORHOODS

Leaving for America
Danzig, Germany
reproduction
YIVO Institute for Jewish Research

Immigrants with the Statue of Liberty
from Yiddish Poster "Food Will Win the War"
New York, 1917
reproduction
National Museum of American Jewish History
Myrna and Ira Brind Purchase Fund

Photograph of Isidor & Chaika Waxman
Kishinev, Russia, ca. 1905
A.Turueprel, photographic studio
reproduction
Courtesy of Helene and Howard Kenvin

Photograph of Isidor and Ida Waxman
New York City, ca. 1910
D. Kerr Studio
reproduction
Courtesy of Helene and Howard Kenvin

Business permit of Chaim Goldstein
Russia, June 20, 1893
National Museum of American Jewish History
Gift of Israel and Bernice Schless

Passport, Stirna Hersheva and family
Dvinsk, Russia, April 4,1905
National Museum of American Jewish History
Gift of Curtis Pontz and Julie Curson in memory of
their father

Silver purse
Russia, ca. 1913
Courtesy of Dr. Arlyn Hochberg Miller

Brass candlesticks of the Shapiro family
Russia, ca. 1900
National Museum of American Jewish History
Gift of Lorna Siegler Miller and Miranda Miller in
memory of Esther Shatz, Irene Asbell and Gertrude
Miller, granddaughters of Shlomo and Gittel Shapiro

Photograph of the Shapiro Family
Russia, 1890
reproduction
National Museum of American Jewish History
Gift of Lorna Siegler Miller and Miranda Miller in
memory of Esther Shatz, Irene Asbell and Gertrude
Miller, granddaughters of Shlomo and Gittel Shapiro

Photograph of Shlomo and Gittel Shapiro
Philadelphia, 1890s
reproduction
National Museum of American Jewish History
Gift of Lorna Siegler Miller and Miranda Miller
in memory of Esther Shatz, Irene Asbell and
Gertrude Miller, granddaughters of Shlomo and
Gittel Shapiro

Tzitzit
owned by Samuel Stein
hand crocheted and embroidered
Poland, ca. 1890
National Museum of American Jewish History
Gift of Gertrude Glaberson

Map of the United States in Yiddish
*Guide to the United States for
the Jewish Immigrant*
by John Carr
published under the auspices of the
Connecticut Daughters of the
American Revolution, 1912
reproduction
National Museum of American Jewish History
Maxwell Whiteman Collection
Purchased by Mr. and Mrs. Stuart Forer
in honor of the 50th wedding anniversary
of Mr. Morris L. and Mrs. Lois G. Forer
Conservation made possible by the Stephen A.
Ritt, Jr. Memorial Fund

Tablets of the Law
Philadelphia, 1918
National Museum of American Jewish History
Gift of Congregation Shaarei Eli
Funds for conservation of the Torah ark were
provided by Jeanne Saligman Levin,
Philadelphia, in loving memory of her mother,
Mary Saligman Levin, and her sister, Augusta
Saligman Levin

Ark curtain
Philadelphia, ca. 1950
National Museum of American Jewish History
Gift of Congregation Shaarei Eli

Hands of Priestly Benediction
Philadelphia, 1918
National Museum of American Jewish History
Gift of Congregation Shaarei Eli

Lions of Judah
Philadelphia, 1917
National Museum of American Jewish History
Gift of Congregation Shaarei Eli

Copper *pushke* (coinholder)
Philadelphia, ca. 1920
National Museum of American Jewish History
Gift of Congregation Shaarei Eli

Roster of Study Groups
Philadelphia, ca. 1930
National Museum of American Jewish History
Gift of Congregation Shaarei Eli

"Blessings at the Reading of the Law"
National Museum of American Jewish History
Gift of Congregation Shaarei Eli

Photograph of Abraham Cahan
New York, 1940
reproduction
Culver Pictures

Yiddish Language typewriter
Hammond Company
Philadelphia, ca. 1925
National Museum of American Jewish History
Gift of Albert and Laura Romm

Banner, Zitomirer Beneficial Society
Philadelphia, 1933
silk with applied paint
National Museum of American Jewish History
Gift of Max Lekoff and Janice L. Booker

Sign for the Workmen's Circle
Passaic, NJ, 1918
wood, handpainted
National Museum of American Jewish History
Gift of Elaine and Stanley Silverman in celebration
of life and community

Strike Poster
Amalgamated Clothing Workers
Philadelphia, ca. 1922
Urban Archives, Temple University

"The Uprising of the Twenty Thousand"
women shirtwaist strikers
New York, 1909
reproduction
Courtesy of Culver Pictures

"The Aims of the Zionist Movement"
poster for Louis Brandeis lecture
Hyperion Theater
Boston, May 9, 1915
Columbia Printing Company
National Museum of American Jewish History
Purchased by Lyn M. and George M. Ross in honor of
Maya Rosenberg's recovery

Lapel pin, Poale Zion Society
Philadelphia Jewish Archives Center

Sons of Zion, Young Judea Club
Philadelphia, 1922
photograph
Philadelphia Jewish Archives Center

Ribbon, Ladies Zion Society
Philadelphia, ca. 1915
Philadelphia Jewish Archives Center

"Monster Protest Meeting Against Suspension of Jewish Immigration into Palestine"
broadside
Boston, May 29, 1930
English and Yiddish
reproduction
National Museum of American Jewish History
Gift of the Anne and John P. McNulty Foundation in
honor of Lyn M. and George M. Ross

Ticket, Grand Ball of the Downtown Zionist District
New York, 1927
National Museum of American Jewish History
Gift of Maxine and Michael Kam

Dance Ticket, Mvasereth Zion Club
New York, 1924
National Museum of American Jewish History
Gift of Maxine and Michael Kam

"I'm Building a Palace in Palestine"
sheet music by Richard Howard, 1916
National Museum of American Jewish History

Ball Ticket, Mvasereth Zion
New York, 1924
National Museum of American Jewish History
Gift of Maxine and Michael Kam

Ticket, United Palestine Appeal Grand Zion Ball
Young Friends of Zion Club
New York, 1927
National Museum of American Jewish History
Gift of Maxine and Michael Kam

Passport, Chava Brucha Baen
Russia, 1913
National Museum of American Jewish History
Gift of Clara K. Braslow in memory of her parents

Cabinet Card portrait of Eva Baen
ca. 1912
reproduction
National Museum of American Jewish History
Gift of Clara K. Braslow in memory of her parents

Needlework Table Runner
by Eva Baen
en route to USA, 1910
National Museum of American Jewish History
Gift of Clara K. Braslow in memory of her parents
Conservation made possible by the Stephen A.
Ritt, Jr. Memorial Fund

Eva Baen with her family
Russia, ca. 1912
cabinet card
reproduction
National Museum of American Jewish History
Gift of Clara K. Braslow in memory of her parents

Eva (Baen) and Louis Kravitz
Philadelphia, ca. 1920
photograph
National Museum of American Jewish History
Gift of Clara K. Braslow in memory of her parents

Night School notebook of Eva Baen
Philadelphia, 1913-1917
H. & P., publishers
National Museum of American Jewish History
Gift of Clara K. Braslow in memory of her
parents

Letter, Eva Baen to "John Vanamaker"
Philadelphia, ca. 1913
reproduction
National Museum of American Jewish History
Gift of Clara K. Braslow in memory
of her parents

Attendance Card of Eva Baen
Kearney Evening Elementary School
Philadelphia, 1914-1915
National Museum of American Jewish History
Gift of Clara K. Braslow in memory
of her parents

The American Citizen
by Reuben Fink
Max M. Maisel, publisher
New York, 1927
National Museum of American Jewish History
Gift of Clara K. Braslow in memory
of her parents

"Many Peoples, One Language"
poster
Cleveland Board of Education, ca. 1917
reproduction
National Museum of American Jewish History
Purchased in memory of Ronald Israelit by the
Robert Saligman Charitable Foundation

Sixth grade graduation
Belmont Elementary School, Philadelphia, 1932
reproduction
National Museum of American Jewish History
Gift of Sylvia Stein

Report cards of Rose Creshkoff
Baugh-Close School
Philadelphia, 1910-1919
Courtesy of Irving and Cyrilla Rosen in memory
of Rose Creshkoff Gaber

Graduation Photograph of Rose Creshkoff
William Penn High School
Philadelphia, 1917
Courtesy of Irving and Cyrilla Rosen in memory
of Rose Creshkoff Gaber

"Jewish Girl Graduates..."
unidentified newsclipping, Philadelphia, 1919
Courtesy of Irving and Cyrilla Rosen in memory
of Rose Creshkoff Gaber

Class photograph, Hebrew Sunday School Society
Philadelphia, 1914
reproduction
National Museum of American Jewish History
Gift of Elaine Weiss

Sunday School medal awarded to Rebecca Neumayer
Hebrew Sunday School Society
Philadephia, June 1, 1884
National Museum of American Jewish History
Gift of Harriet M. Lichtenstein

"History of the United States"
anti-Semitic postcard
National Museum of American Jewish History

"Our flag"
anti-Semitic postcard
National Museum of American Jewish History

The Protocols of the Learned Elders of Zion
translated by Victor E. Marsden
The Patriotic Publishing Co.
Chicago, 1934
National Museum of American Jewish History

"The Attitude of the Knights of the Ku Klux Klan Toward the Jew"
by H.W. Evans
ca. 1924
pamphlet
National Museum of American Jewish History

"Am I An Anti-Semite?"
radio adresses by Rev. Charles E. Coughlin
Condon Printing Company, Detroit
November 6, 1938-January 1, 1939
National Museum of American Jewish History
Myrna and Ira Brind Purchase Fund

Social Justice
Rev. Charles E. Coughlin, editor
Vol. 2A, no. 23, December 5, 1938
printed in Royal Oak, Michigan
National Museum of American Jewish History

The Dearborn Independent
Henry Ford, publisher
William J. Cameron, editor
Michigan, September 22, 1923
Dearborn, Michigan
National Museum of American Jewish History

Pop-up New Year's Greeting card
Germany, early 20th c.
National Museum of American Jewish History
Mr. and Mrs. Howard Yusem Purchase Fund

"A Small Wedding, But a Happy One"
Der Groyser Kundes, New York, 1911
reproduction
Courtesy of Peter H. Schweitzer

Advertising flyer
Jean's Service Bureau
Worcester, Massachusetts, early 20th c.
reproduction
National Museum of American Jewish History
Purchased by Margo Bloom in honor
of Elaine Silverman
Conservation made possible by the Stephen A.
Ritt, Jr. Memorial Fund

"Rabbi Snapir's Wedding Salon"
advertising sign
Philadelphia, ca. 1910
National Museum of American Jewish History
Gift of Morton "Moe" Tener in honor of Beth Sholom

Cigar Box
Wedding of Dr. Abraham Moss to Ethel Plotz
Hotel St. Regis, New York, June 23, 1914
Courtesy of Peter H. Schweitzer

Ketubbah
Frank Zimring and Anna Brenner
New York, December 31, 1911
Courtesy of Peter H. Schweitzer

Wedding Dress of Fannie Goodman
Philadelphia, December 20, 1911
National Museum of American Jewish History
Gift of Reti Kornfeld

Ketubah of Ida Einbinder and Jacob Weisenthal
New York, March 25, 1917
reproduction
Courtesy of Helene and Howard Kenvin

Butter chiller
Czechoslovakia, ca. 1917
cut glass
Courtesy of Helene and Howard Kenvin

Wedding portrait of Albert and Rose Blum
Philadelphia, July 1910
National Museum of American Jewish History
Gift of Esther Blum
Conservation in memory of Claire Blum
Schwartz, devoted Museum shop volunteer
Conservation made possible by the Stephen A.
Ritt, Jr. Memorial Fund

Bow tie of Albert Blum
Philadelphia, July 10, 1910
National Museum of American Jewish History
Gift of Esther Blum

Gloves of Albert Blum
Philadelphia, July 10, 1910
National Museum of American Jewish History
Gift of Esther Blum
Conservation made possible by the Stephen A.
Ritt, Jr. Memorial Fund

**Wedding invitation of Albert Blum
and Rose Schwartz**
Philadelphia, July 10, 1910
National Museum of American Jewish History
Gift of Esther Blum

MODERN COMMUNITIES

The S.S. St. Louis in Havana Harbor
Havana, Cuba, June 3, 1939
reproduction
Wide World Photos, Inc.

Letter, Hamburg-Amerika Line
To "Herr Josef Joseph"
Amsterdam, April 14, 1939
Courtesy of Liesl Joseph Loeb

Value Declaration
Hamburg, 1939
Courtesy of Liesl Joseph Loeb

Postcard of S.S. St. Louis
1939
Courtesy of Liesl Joseph Loeb

Steamer trunk of Josef Joseph
National Museum of American Jewish History
Gift of Barry S. and Joan C. Slosberg

Passport
Lilly Joseph
Germany, May 2, 1939
Courtesy of Liesl Joseph Loeb

Passport
Josef Joseph
Germany, May 2, 1939
Courtesy of Liesl Joseph Loeb

Joseph family quota number
Germany, August 20, 1938
Courtesy of Liesl Joseph Loeb

Members of the Passenger Committee
1939
reproduction
Courtesy of Liesl Joseph Loeb

Joseph family luggage tags
May 5, 1939
Courtesy of Liesl Joseph Loeb

Passenger baggage claim ticket
Havana, 1939
Courtesy of Liesl Joseph Loeb

Cable to Prime Minister Chamberlain from "Passengers on the St. Louis"
reproduction
United States Holocaust Memorial Museum

Letter from Liesl Joseph to Morris Troper
S.S. St. Louis, June 17, 1939
reproduction
United States Holocaust Memorial Museum

Liesl Joseph with flowers from Morris Troper
June, 1939
reproduction
Courtesy of Liesl Joseph Loeb

Cable from Editor of *News Chronicle* to St. Louis
London, June 13, 1939
reproduction
United States Holocaust Memorial Museum

Refugees in Havana Harbor
June 3, 1939
reproduction
Associated Press

Miss America, 1945
Bess Myerson
Alfred Eisenstaedt, photographer
reproduction
Courtesy of Bess Myerson

Hank Greenberg wins the pennant
Detroit, 1945
reproduction
New York Times Pictures

The Greene Family
Flushing, NY, May 1941
photograph
American Jewish Historical Society
New York City, NY and Waltham, MA
Gift of Lois Greene Stone

"My Confirmation"
photograph album of Lois Greene
Flushing, NY
June 6, 1948
American Jewish Historical Society
New York City, NY and Waltham, MA
Gift of Lois Greene Stone

Confirmation certificate of Lois Greene
Flushing Jewish Center
Flushing, NY, April 28, 1948
American Jewish Historical Society
New York City, NY and Waltham, MA
Gift of Lois Greene Stone

Lois Greene's graduation photograph
January 1948
American Jewish Historical Society
New York City, NY and Waltham, MA
Gift of Lois Greene Stone

Diary of Lois Greene
Flushing, NY, 1946
American Jewish Historical Society
New York City, NY and Waltham, MA
Gift of Lois Greene Stone

Lois Greene at summer camp
Camp Watitoh, Massachusetts
August 1951
photograph
American Jewish Historical Society
New York City, NY and Waltham, MA
Gift of Lois Greene Stone

Swimming card of Lois Greene
The American National Red Cross
August 25, 1949
American Jewish Historical Society
New York City, NY and Waltham, MA
Gift of Lois Greene Stone

"Watitoh Watchtower"
Camp Watitoh, Massachusetts
August 12, 1951
American Jewish Historical Society
New York City, NY and Waltham, MA
Gift of Lois Greene Stone

Postcard of Temple Beth Sholom
Miami Beach, FL
Percival Goodman, architect
Frank Boran, photographer
National Museum of American Jewish History
Purchased in honor of Jeanne Schwartzman's
90th birthday by her colleagues in the
Museum shop

Postcard of Temple Beth Zion
Buffalo, NY
Don Glena, photographer
printed by Ernest Gunzburger
National Museum of American Jewish History
Purchased in honor of Jeanne Schwartzman's
90th birthday by her colleagues in the
Museum shop

"Arise and Build"
fundraising tile
reproduction
North Shore Congregation Israel

Postcard of "Beautiful Temple Emanu-El"
Palm Beach, FL
Mort Kayne Studio, photographer
National Museum of American Jewish History
Purchased in honor of Jeanne Schwartzman's
birthday by her colleagues in the Museum shop

Letter, Rabbi Mortimer Cohen to
Frank Lloyd Wright
Philadelphia, November 16, 1953
Congregation Beth Sholom Archives

Sketch of ark for Beth Sholom Synagogue
Rabbi Mortimer Cohen
1953
Congregation Beth Sholom Archives

Interior of Beth Sholom Synagogue
reproduction
Courtesy of Balthazar Korab

Telegram, Frank Lloyd Wright to
Rabbi Mortimer Cohen
Phoenix, Arizona
February 6, 1954
Congregation Beth Sholom Archives

Map of Israel
used in Temple Oheb Shalom school
Salem, New Jersey
National Museum of American Jewish History
Conservation made possible by the Stephen A.
Ritt, Jr. Memorial Fund

Classroom at Har Zion Hebrew School
Philadelphia, late 1940s
reproduction
Har Zion Temple Archives

Hebrew school notebook
Moshe Green, publisher
1952
National Museum of American Jewish History

Sisterhood gift shop
Philadelphia
photograph
Reform Congregation Keneseth Israel Archives

"Sisterhood Prayers for All Occasions"
Women's Branch, Union of Orthodox Jewish
Congregations of America
American Jewish Historical Society
New York City, NY and Waltham, MA

Kiddush cup
Daniel Blumberg, artist
1966
handmade silver, gold and enamel
Presented by the Sisterhood to Reform Congregation
Keneseth Israel
Temple Judea Museum of Keneseth Israel

Poster, "Look what $3 Buys you..."
Keneseth Israel Sisterhood, Philadelphia, 1940s
reproduction
Reform Congregation Keneseth Israel Archives

Ahavath Achim Ladies Auxiliary Cookbook
Fairfield, CT, 1968
National Museum of American Jewish History

Koch and Kvell
cookbook
B'nai Abraham Sisterhood
Easton, PA, 1968
National Museum of American Jewish History

Treasures from our Kitchens
cookbook
Beth Am Sisterhood
Cleveland Heights, Ohio
National Museum of American Jewish History

Hadassah Cookbook
Pittsfield, Massachusetts, 1945
National Museum of American Jewish History

Food for Fun
cookbook
B'nai B'rith Women
New York, New York, 1957
National Museum of American Jewish History

What's cooking in Council
cookbook
Asbury Park, NJ, 1949
National Museum of American Jewish History

Scrapbook
Har Zion Sisterhood
1971-1972
Har Zion Temple Archives

"Or Hadash" ("A New Light")
newsletter
Vol. 2, No. 1, Hanukkah 5726
reproduction
Har Zion Radnor Sisterhood, Philadelphia
Har Zion Temple Archives

Bar Mitzvah invitation
Norman Paul
Philadelphia, January 6, 1951
reproduction
National Museum of American Jewish History
Gift of Norman and Charlotte Paul

Bar Mitzvah invitation
Alan Goodman
Philadelphia, November 9, 1946
National Museum of American Jewish History
Gift of Gwen and Alan Goodman

Photograph album
Alan Goodman
Philadelphia, November 9, 1946
Courtesy of Alan Goodman

Donna Forman's Bat Mitzvah
Hollis Hills Jewish Center, Queens, New York
November 29, 1963
photograph
reproduction
Courtesy of Donna Forman

Bar Mitzvah invitation
Nelson Braslow
Philadelphia, July 4, 1963
National Museum of American Jewish History
Gift of Clara K. Braslow

"Nelson's Bar Mitzvah"
matchbook
satin with embossed lettering
National Museum of American Jewish History
Gift of Clara K. Braslow

"Prayers, Blessings and Hymns"
compiled and arranged by Rabbi C.M. Brecher
Rosenberg Hebrew Books, July 4, 1963
white leatherette, gold stamped
National Museum of American Jewish History
Gift of Clara K. Braslow

Bar Mitzvah cards
Nelson Braslow
Philadelphia, July 4, 1963
National Museum of American Jewish History
Gift of Clara K. Braslow

**Memento from Louis Rosenberg's
Bar Mitzvah**
Philadelphia, September 28, 1969
ceramic plate with phototransfers
National Museum of American Jewish History

Pink satin dress and hat
ca. 1955
National Museum of American Jewish History
Gift of Meyer H. and Sophie M. Sklar

"Life Goes to a Bar Mitzvah"
Life magazine, October 13, 1952
Vol. 33, no. 15
National Museum of American Jewish History
Purchased by the Museum staff in recognition
of the dedication and commitment of our
volunteers

Bat Mitzvah certificate
Helene Kenvin
Kew Gardens Hills, New York
December 17, 1954
reproduction
Courtesy of Helene and Howard Kenvin

The Jewish Home Beautiful
Betty D. Greenberg and Althea O. Silverman
Published by the National Women's League
of the United Synagogue of America
New York, 1953
Courtesy of Helene and Howard Kenvin

**Letter, Abraham Wolper to the School
Committee**
Chelsea, MA
December 3, 1949
reproduction
American Jewish Historical Society
New York City, NY and Waltham, MA

**"Public Hearing Set as Mother
Hits Carol-Singing in Schools"**
unidentified newsclipping
reproduction
American Jewish Historical Society
New York City, NY and Waltham, MA

**"Seek to Ban Singing of Carols in
Public Schools"**
newsclipping, Boston, MA
December, 1949
reproduction
American Jewish Historical Society
New York City, NY and Waltham, MA

**Letter to "Dear Mrs. Wolpert"
[sic] from "A Jewish Mother"**
December, 1949
reproduction
American Jewish Historical Society
New York City, NY and Waltham, MA

Letter to Abraham Wolper and Goldie Roller
Chelsea, Mass.
December, 1949
reproduction
American Jewish Historical Society
New York City, New York and Waltham,
Massachusetts

Letter to "My dear Mrs. Wolper"
Harry L. Kohn
McKeesport, PA
December 9, 1949
reproduction
American Jewish Historical Society
New York City, NY and Waltham, MA

**Letter, Mr. Abraham Wolper to
Mr. Howard L. Ostler**
Chelsea School Committee
December 9, 1949
reproduction
American Jewish Historical Society
New York City, NY and Waltham, MA

**Letter from "Good Americans
and Good Christians"**
December 12, 1949
reproduction
American Jewish Historical Society
New York City, NY and Waltham, MA

"Happy Hanukkah" decoration
ca. 1970
Courtesy of Rebekah Sobel

Hanukkah candles
National Museum of American Jewish History
Gift of Maxine and Michael Kam

"Menora-Lite"
electrified Hanukkah menorah
ca. 1955
Courtesy of Leonard Bisk

"The Maccabee"
North Bergen, NJ, 1950s
reproduction
Dra-Dell Corporation, photographers
YIVO Institute for Jewish Research

Hanukkah Celebration
Har Zion Temple
Philadelphia
photograph
reproduction
Har Zion Temple Archives

Hanukkah coloring book
National Museum of American Jewish History
Anne Opstbaum Memorial Fund

Chanukah Fun and Story Book
K'tav Publishing House, 1952
Har Zion Temple Archives

"Chanukah Music Box"
record album
Kinor records, 1951
National Museum of American Jewish History

Dreidels
Courtesy of Rebekah Sobel

**Martin Luther King, Jr. and
Abraham Joshua Heschel**
photograph, 1965
reproduction
American Jewish Archives

Andrew Goodman in training
Oxford, Ohio, 1964
photograph
reproduction
Courtesy of Dr. Carolyn Goodman

Postcard, Andrew Goodman to his parents
Meridian, Mississippi
June 21, 1964
Courtesy of Dr. Carolyn Goodman

Scrapbook from the Selma march
January–March, 1965
Courtesy of Roy Mersky

Name Tag
SNCC (Student Non-Violent
Coordinating Committee)
Fall conference
Atlanta, Georgia, October 14-16, 1960
Courtesy of Martin Oppenheimer

Membership cards
CORE (Congress of Racial Equality)
Philadelphia chapter
1963-64
Courtesy of Martin Oppenheimer

Civil Rights demonstration
Philadelphia, 1960
photograph
reproduction
Courtesy of Martin Oppenheimer

"A Manual for Direct Action"
Martin Oppenheimer and George Lakey
Princeton, N.J., 1967
Courtesy of Martin Oppenheimer

NEW IDENTITIES

Coinholder
Children's Forest in Yakinton
Jewish National Fund
1966
National Museum of American Jewish History

Tree planting certificate
Jewish National Fund
June 11, 1961
National Museum of American Jewish History
Gift of Robert and Molly Freedman

At the Western Wall
Jerusalem, 1967
reproduction
Corbis-Bettman

Moshe Dayan, Yitzhak Rabin and Rahavan Zeen
Jerusalem, 1967
reproduction
Corbis-Bettman

Advertisement for Rally
reproduced from the *Jewish Exponent*, June 9, 1967
National Museum of American Jewish History

Postcard, Zitomerer Beneficial Association
Philadelphia, June 7, 1967
reproduction
National Museum of American Jewish History
Gift of Janice Booker and Max Lekoff

"We're Not Alone"
cartoon, 1967
Noah Bee, artist
ink on paper
National Museum of American Jewish History
Gift of Marian Bee, Carmi Bee, and Sharon
Herman in memory of their husband/father,
Noah Bee

Jewish Exponent
Philadelphia, June 16, 1967
National Museum of American Jewish History

Interior of Havurat Shalom
Somerville, Massachusetts
reproduction
Courtesy of David Kronfeld

imhat Torah celebration
Congregation P'nai Or
Philadelphia, July, 1987
reproduction
Courtesy of P'nai Or Religious Fellowship

Exterior of Havurat Shalom
Somerville, MA, 1972
reproduction
Courtesy of Richard Siegel

"Havurat Shalom Community Seminary"
flyer, 1968
Courtesy of Dr. Arthur Green

Kippah **worn by Richard Siegel**
crocheted by Bluma Stoller
Camp Ramah, 1969
Courtesy of Richard Siegel

Vision statements
by James Sleeper, Art Green, Kathy Green and Epi
[Seymour Epstein]
reproductions
Courtesy of Richard Siegel

"Help us Create a Jewish Whole Earth Catalogue"
flyer
Courtesy of Richard Siegel

The Jewish Catalog
compiled and edited by Richard Siegel, Michael
Strassfeld, and Sharon Strassfeld
Philadelphia: The Jewish Publication Society, 1973
National Museum of American Jewish History
Gift of Karen Mittelman

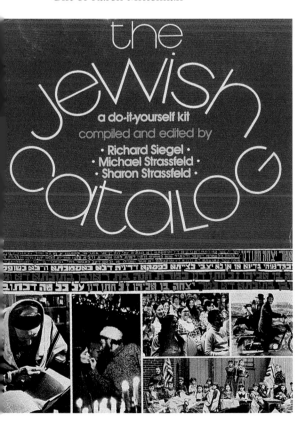

Letter to the editors
by Karen Mittelman
Virginia, June 11, 1975
reproduction
Courtesy of Richard Siegel

Letter to the editors
by Arthur Spitzer
New Haven, CT, March 10, 1974
reproduction
Courtesy of Richard Siegel

Letter to the editors
by Art Brown
Philadelphia, PA, n.d.
reproduction
Courtesy of Richard Siegel

Letter to the editors
by Rabbi Gershom Schusterman
Long Beach, CA, April 26, 1974
reproduction
Courtesy of Richard Siegel

"Jewish Students Rap their Elders"
The Washington Post, March 10, 1969
reproduction
Courtesy of Mike Tabor

Poster for *Fabrangen*
1971-72
Courtesy of Mike Tabor

"*Fabrangen***: A Jewish FREE Cultural Center"**
flyer, 1971-72
reproduction
Courtesy of Mike Tabor

Cap with protest buttons
worn by Arthur Waskow to demonstrations
Courtesy of Rabbi Arthur Waskow

Flyer for the Poor People's Campaign
April 1968
reproduction
Courtesy of Mike Tabor

Vigil for Peace outside the White House
The Washington Post, December 13, 1969
(Jews for Urban Justice reprint)
reproduction
Courtesy of Mike Tabor

Picket sign
"Jews for Urban Justice"
reproduction
Courtesy of Mike Tabor

"The Jewish Urban Guerilla"
newsletter
Volume 111, No. 7
October 1970
reproduction
Courtesy of Mike Tabor

Picket sign, "Mr. Danzansky, There's BLOOD on every grape sold!"
Jews for Urban Justice, 1968-69
reproduction
Courtesy of Mike Tabor

Picket sign, "Don't Buy California Grapes"
United Farm Workers Organizing Committee, 1968-69
Courtesy of Mike Tabor

Bumper sticker, "Boycott Grapes!"
Courtesy of Mike Tabor

"No, it's not the Jewish People this time. . ."
flyer for Tisha B'av gathering, July 1972
reproduction
Courtesy of Mike Tabor

"Trees and Life for Vietnam"
brochure, early 1970s
Courtesy of Mike Tabor

"A Jewish Campaign for the People's Peace Treaty"
brochure, early 1970s
Courtesy of Mike Tabor

"The Freedom Seder"
by Arthur Waskow
Micah Press, 1969
Courtesy of Rabbi Arthur Waskow

Photograph of the first Freedom Seder
Lincoln Temple
Washington, DC
April 4, 1969
reproduction
Courtesy of Rabbi Arthur Waskow

Feminist Passover Seder
New York City, 1991
reproduction
Courtesy of Joan Roth, photographer

***Ms.* magazine**
Volume 1, no. 6
December, 1972
National Museum of American Jewish History

***LILITH*, the Jewish Feminist Magazine**
No. 6
Lilith Publications, Inc.
New York, 1979/5740
Courtesy of *LILITH* magazine

Rabbi Sally Priesand
photograph, 1972
reproduction
Hebrew Union College Archives

Reading the Torah
International Conference on Feminism and
Orthodoxy
New York City, February 1997
Courtesy of Joan Roth, photographer

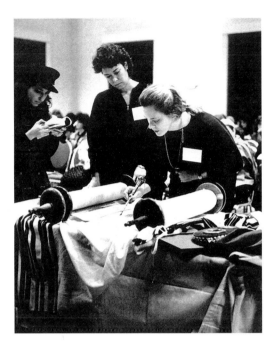

"Taking Our Place at Sinai: Women Stitch Torah"
quilt stitched by the women members of P'nai Or
Philadelphia, PA, 1997
co-visioned by Genie Budow and Elizheva Hurvich
Courtesy P'nai Or Religious Fellowship

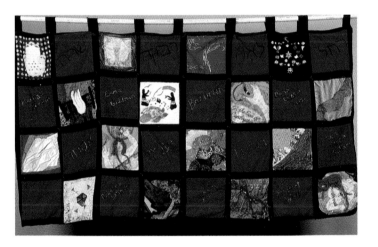

"Miriam's Cup: Rise Up"
Susan Duhan Felix
Berkeley, CA, 1997
pit fired ceramic
National Museum of American Jewish History
Gift of Barbara Dobkin

"Shoshanah II"
Tallit for a woman cantor
Renee Goldin Fischman, 1992
silk, cotton lace and metallic silk trim
embroidered and appliqued
National Museum of American Jewish History
Contemporary Artifacts Purchase Fund

"Soviet Jews - Demand Their Freedom!"
placard
National Museum of American Jewish History
Gift of David and Elaine Ravich

Protest for Soviet Jews
New York City, May 31, 1981
reproduction
American Jewish Historical Society
New York City, NY and Waltham, MA

Philadelphia activists at the Western Wall
Jerusalem, 1978
photograph
reproduction
Courtesy of Constance and Joseph Smukler

Connie Smukler
Women's Plea for Soviet Jewry conference
Old Christ Church, Philadelphia, 1976
photograph
reproduction
Courtesy of Constance and Joseph Smukler

"Route to Freedom"
board game
The Board of Jewish Education, 1976
Courtesy of Constance and Joseph Smukler

Tote bag
National Museum of American Jewish History
Gift of Lorna Adelman

"No Ransom For Soviet Jews"
"Free Soviet Jews"
pinback buttons
National Museum of American Jewish History
Gift of Lorna Adelman

"Protest Oppression of Soviet Jewry"
stamps
National Museum of American Jewish History
Gift of Lorna Adelman

Prisoner-of-conscience bracelet
for Yaakov Levin
National Museum of American Jewish History
Gift of Lorna Adelman

Return receipt cards
U.S. Postal Service, 1980s
National Museum of American Jewish History
Gift of Lorna Adelman

Irma Chernyak with the Smuklers
Leningrad, 1974
photograph
Courtesy of Constance and Joseph Smukler

Delegate's badge
Constance Smukler
2nd World Conference on Soviet Jewry
Brussels, Belgium, 1976
Courtesy of Constance and Joseph Smukler

Delegate's badge
Joseph Smukler
2nd World Conference on Soviet Jewry
Brussels, Belgium, 1976
Courtesy of Constance and Joseph Smukler

Holocaust Remembrance Service
Temple Emanuel, New York, 1991
reproduction
Courtesy of Joan Roth, photographer

Report of the President's Commission on the Holocaust
presented by Elie Wiesel, Chairman
September 27, 1979
National Museum of American Jewish History
Gift of David and Elaine Ravich

"Holocaust Torah Dedication" poster
Temple Beth Hillel/Beth EL
Wynnewood, PA, March 19, 1995
reproduction
National Museum of American Jewish History
Gift of Tempel Beth Hillel/Beth El

Program booklet
Holocaust Torah dedication
Temple Beth Hillel/Beth El
Wynnewood, PA, March 19, 1995
National Museum of American Jewish History
Gift of Temple Beth Hillel/Beth El

Song sheet
Holocaust Torah dedication
Temple Beth Hillel/Beth El
Wynnewood, PA, March 19, 1995
reproduction
National Museum of American Jewish History
Gift of Temple Beth Hillel/Beth El

Photographs of Holocaust Torah dedication
Temple Beth Hillel/Beth El
Wynnewood, PA, March 19, 1995
reproductions
National Museum of American Jewish History
Gift of Beth Hillel/Beth El

Paper crown
Holocaust Torah dedication
Temple Beth Hillel/Beth El
Wynnewood, PA, March 19, 1995
National Museum of American Jewish History
Gift of Temple Beth Hillel/Beth El

List of Lenders to the Exhibition

American Jewish Historical Society,
Waltham, Massachusetts and New York, New York

American Jewish Archives, Cincinnati, Ohio

Associated Press, New York

Beck Archives of Rocky Mountain Jewish History, Center for Judaic Studies
and Penrose Library, University of Denver

Beth Sholom Congregation, Elkins Park, Pennsylvania

Corbis-Bettman Archives, New York

Leonard Bisk, Ithaca, New York

Center for Southwest Research, Zimmerman Library,
University of New Mexico, Albuquerque

Colorado Historical Society, Denver, Colorado

Culver Pictures, New York

Denver Public Library, Denver, Colorado

Fray Angelico Chavez History Library, Palace of the Governors,
Museum of New Mexico, Santa Fe

Georgia Historical Society, Savannah, Georgia

Dr. Carolyn Goodman, New York

Gwen and Alan Goodman, Penn Valley, Pennsylvania

Dr. Arthur Green, Newton Centre, Massachusetts

John Hopf Photography, Newport, Rhode Island

Har Zion Temple, Penn Valley, Pennsylvania

Hebrew Union College Skirball Cultural Center, Los Angeles, California

Marjorie Hornbein, Denver, Colorado

Helene and Howard Kenvin, Esopus, New York

David Kronfeld, New York

Library Company of Philadelphia

Library of Congress, Washington, D.C.

Liesl Joseph Loeb, Elkins Park, Pennsylvania

Lilith: The Jewish Feminist Magazine, New York

Robert Marcus, Springfield, Virginia

List of Lenders to the Exhibition

Roy Mersky, Austin, Texas

Congregation Mickve Israel, Savannah, Georgia

Congregation Mikveh Israel, Philadelphia

Arlyn H. Miller, Philadelphia

Museum of the City of New York, New York

Newport Historical Society, Newport, Rhode Island

New York Times Photo Archives, New York

New York Historical Society, New York

North Shore Congregation Israel, Glencoe, Illinois

Martin Oppenheimer, Princeton, New Jersey

Palace of the Governors Collection, Museum of New Mexico, Santa Fe

Beth Shepherd Peters, New York

Photo Archives, Palace of the Governors, Museum of New Mexico, Santa Fe

Philadelphia Jewish Archives Center, Philadelphia

P'nai Or Religious Fellowship, Philadelphia

David and Elaine Ravich, Del Ray Beach, Florida

Reform Congregation Keneseth Israel Archives, Elkins Park, Pennsylvania

Irving and Cyrilla Rosen, Lafayetteville, Pennsylvania

Joan Roth, New York

Peter H. Schweitzer, New York

Sharon Seeman, Littleton, Colorado

Richard Siegel, New York

Rebekah Sobel, Philadelphia

Constance and Joseph Smukler, Philadelphia

Mike Tabor, Takoma Park, Maryland

Temple University Urban Archives, Philadelphia

United States Holocaust Memorial Museum, Washington, D.C.

Rabbi Arthur Waskow, Philadelphia

Wide World Photos, Inc., New York

YIVO Institute for Jewish Research, New York